Sold into Marriage

A survivor of a bizarre [...] incredible story to jou[...] unique, harrowing tale, [...] terrible events. It is the story of a young girl used by old men for their own needs – sex, power and money. She could be a real-life Sive, from John B Keane's famous play. But her story did not happen in the 1950s, it happened in the modern Ireland of the 1970s. This woman is still in her early forties. From the depths of despair she has won back her integrity, her identity and her sense of humour.

THIS IS A TRUE STORY

'A disturbing and well-written account of savage cruelty'
The Sunday Tribune

'A chilling account of cruelty, abuse and domination.
Nuala comes across as an exceptional person who, despite her
horrific ordeal, never lost her sense of self' *Ireland on Sunday*

'A sad reminder of the closed society which we tolerated
until very recently' *Leinster Leader*

'An incredible and disturbing story' *Southside People*

SEAN BOYNE

Born in Dublin, Sean has worked all his life
in journalism. He is currently political editor with
the *Sunday World*, one of Ireland's major newspapers.
He also co-authored, with Peter O'Neill, a biography
of the racehorse trainer Paddy Mullins.

SOLD INTO MARRIAGE

SEAN BOYNE

THE O'BRIEN PRESS
DUBLIN

First published 1998 by The O'Brien Press Ltd,
20 Victoria Road, Dublin 6, Ireland.
Tel: +353 1 4923333; Fax: +353 1 4922777
E-mail: books@obrien.ie
Website: www.obrien.ie
Reprinted 1998 (twice), 2000, 2002, 2003.

ISBN 0-86278-581-2

British Library Cataloguing-in-Publication Data
Boyne, Sean
Sold into marriage : one girl's living nightmare
1.Marriage - Ireland 2.Wife abuse - Ireland 3.Ireland - Biography
I.Title
306.8'092

6 7 8 9 10
03 04 05 06 07

Editing, typesetting, layout, design: The O'Brien Press Ltd
Printing: Bookmarque Ltd

CONTENTS

Introduction *page 7*

1 The Ceremony *9*

2 The Match *16*

3 The Seller of Dreams *28*

4 The Courtship *39*

5 The Escape Attempt *64*

6 The Newly-Weds *76*

7 The Price *93*

8 The Beatings *107*

9 The Police *117*

10 The Pregnancy *133*

11 The Birth *142*

12 The Escape *155*

13 The Last Visit *173*

Epilogue *184*

NOTE

The Irish woman whose story is told in the pages that follow is a rape victim. When the woman I call 'Nuala' was forced as a sixteen-year-old by her father to marry an elderly farmer in the 1970s, there was no offence in Irish law known as marital rape. A husband could force his wife to have sexual intercourse, and it was not a crime. The law has since been changed, and marital rape is now a serious offence in Ireland.

Despite assurances that this would be a marriage of convenience with no sex involved, the teenage bride found herself in a nightmare world in which she was tied down and raped, and beaten repeatedly.

Of course, in terms of Irish law in the 1970s, Nuala was never raped, as the deed happened within marriage, albeit a forced marriage. Yet in moral terms, she is very definitely a rape victim, and for the sake of her children would like to avail of the anonymity that is the traditional prerogative of the woman who suffers this most serious of crimes against the person.

In deference to her wishes, all names of individuals have been changed in this book, as have the names of towns and villages. Some details have also been changed to protect her identity and that of certain other individuals who were caught up in this saga. Some of the conversations reported in this book should not be taken as verbatim accounts of what was actually said at the time – nobody took notes. However, the dialogue and narrative convey the general flavour of the events as remembered by Nuala.

INTRODUCTION

It took her more than twenty-two years to get in touch. I can't honestly say I spent all that time waiting for her call. Even though I had never forgotten about her and her horrific story, I never dreamt our paths would cross again. And then, when I was least expecting it, the phone rang. It was a Friday afternoon in June 1997. At first, it seemed like one of those routine calls that are part and parcel of the daily grind of Irish newspaper life. A woman was on the line. Sounding hesitant and rather tense, she said she wanted to tell the story of her life. I have to admit I was sceptical. From time to time, members of the public phone newspapers to seek to tell their life story, even though they may have little to tell. I asked the woman if there was anything unusual about her life. There was a pause. Then she said that when she was sixteen she was sold by her father as a bride to an elderly man.

For a moment I was dumbstruck. I knew immediately that this was the story that had been on my mind on and off for more than two decades. Back in the mid-1970s I had written a story for the *Sunday World* newspaper about a sixteen-year-old girl who had tried to commit suicide after being forced by her father to marry a farmer four times her age. The farmer had, in effect, bought her. The story did not go into any great detail, and only covered the broad outline of the affair. The information came from a confidential source. Those involved were not named, but the girl later wrote to the paper denying the story. I figured she had written the letter under duress. I never met her and often wondered what had happened to her. The frightening details stuck in my mind, but I realised that the chances of getting to talk to her were extremely remote. And now, after all those years, she was on the line. I knew that this had to be the woman whose story had made such a lasting impression upon me.

I felt as if the hair was standing out on the back of my neck as I took the phone call in the Dublin newsroom of the *Sunday World*. I said to the caller, 'I think I know who you are.' I asked if she was from a particular village, and she confirmed that she was.

She mentioned her name and I immediately recognised it. She told me, 'Your newspaper ran a story about my case many years ago.' I replied, 'I know. It was I who wrote it.'

CHAPTER ONE

THE CEREMONY

She sat stiffly in her wedding dress in the back seat of her father's beat-up Anglia. Her mother sat quietly beside her. Her father heaved himself in behind the wheel, grinning at the neighbours who had come out to wave them off to the church. He turned the key in the ignition two or three times and finally the engine coughed into life with a husky, asthmatic roar. Dan Slowney, in his best suit and with his hair slicked back, puffing on an untipped Player, confidently steered the car slowly away from his cottage on the main street of Knockslattery village.

Nuala's thoughts were in turmoil. She found it hard to focus on what was happening to her. She was in a daze. It was good that her mother was there with her, but she could sense her mother's unhappiness and tension too. She knew her mother could not do anything for her now. Nuala looked at her father and thought how she loathed him.

Every neighbour in the tiny, rundown village set amid rolling hills and farmland seemed to be out on the street. They were waving and calling out their best wishes. Children, laughing and shouting, ran alongside the car. Then Nuala spotted her three friends standing on the opposite side of the street in their summer dresses, near the tiny stone-built national school where they had all attended classes. The teenage girls, Carmel, Grace and Pauline, stood apart from everybody else and looked frightened. Their eyes were red, as if they had been crying. One of them nodded at Nuala. Another girl, Nuala's very best friend Carmel, raised her hand weakly as if to say goodbye. They were not sharing in the festivities. They knew the real story. It was as if they were at a funeral, not a wedding.

Nuala glanced quickly at her pals and looked away again. She knew if their eyes met for too long she would break down. It was bad enough being a spectacle in her wedding dress in front of the neighbours. She didn't want to cry in front of them as well. She tried to remain inscrutable, but she reckoned that anybody who looked closely into her eyes would see her terror and despair.

She hated all this unwanted attention from the neighbours, and just wanted to get out of there as quickly as possible. They had only travelled a couple of hundred yards when she heard the engine spluttering and falling away into an ominous silence, as the car coasted to a stop. The grin froze on Dan's face.

'Ah for Jaysus sake, what's wrong with the shaggin' thing now?' he fumed as he jumped out of the car.

'Oh my God,' groaned Nuala through gritted teeth to her mother. 'Why couldn't he hire a big black wedding car like everybody else?' Her mother reached out and gripped her hand, to reassure her. Nuala felt trapped in front of all these people gawping at her.

She said to her mother, 'I'm not pushing it, Mammy. I don't care what he says, I'm not getting out to push it. Not in my wedding dress.'

The car happened to give up the ghost in front of the village water pump. Some people in the rural Ireland of the time still did not have running water and would get their supply from the pump. A cousin of her father's happened to be filling milk churns with water for household use. Dan quickly roped him in, and the churns were hastily pulled out from the back seat of the cousin's Mini. Nuala and her parents squeezed into the small car and the cousin, a man called Tommy, set off for the church. Dan was grinning again, puffing confidently on his ever-present cigarette. Another problem solved, no bother.

Nuala could sense Tommy's coolness towards Dan. She reckoned that Tommy had heard through his family connections about the marriage and that he did not approve. Tommy was a decent man and his reserve towards her father was a gesture that she appreciated. Fair play to you, Tommy, she thought.

'Will you come around to the hotel later for a few jars, Tommy?' said Dan as they arrived at the church.

'I'll talk to herself and we'll see if we can make it,' said Tommy. Nuala knew he wouldn't show up.

It was a small country church, set in tranquil, open countryside, serving a small farming community. Generations of dead from the locality lay beneath carved stone Celtic crosses in the adjoining graveyard, with the soft green outline of distant hills on the horizon. It was neither her parish church nor the groom's. She didn't fully understand why it had to be this particular church. All kinds of arrangements were made without her knowledge, and the selection of the church was one of them. She did not know what procedures were followed to arrange the ceremony, but has a vague recollection of forms being filled in to pave the way for a wedding outside her own parish.

Only Nuala's close relatives were at the nuptials. The groom's family did not attend – his grown-up children did not approve of the match. Dan led his daughter down the aisle and in front of the altar she joined husband-to-be Paddy McGorril, whom she had known only a few weeks, had met about half a dozen times and with whom she had never even had a proper conversation. This man, with whom she was supposed to spend the rest of her married life until death claimed one or other of them, was a virtual stranger to her. She was sixteen; he was in his mid-sixties. And then there were those rumours she had heard about him, rumours that frightened her.

The church wasn't packed but she could sense all those strangers there, all looking at her. She felt as if their stares were burning into her back. She felt like turning around to them and saying, 'Would ye ever buzz off and mind your own business!' She could hear the usual sounds of a congregation in a small country church – the echoing coughs, the whispers, the rattle of shoes on the floor. She knew in her heart they were not all there just for the Mass. They were there for the spectacle. Word had gone around that a schoolgirl was marrying an elderly man. People were paying into the Olympia Theatre up in Dublin for less. She could imagine elderly women in hats and scarves whispering to each other and blessing themselves, and glancing at prayer books – and craning their necks for a glimpse of the odd couple at the top of the church.

She had a feeling of doom, a sense of foreboding, as she knelt at the altar. Her emotions were a turbulent mixture of disgust, fear, and hatred. She just did not want to be here, with this man whom she detested. There were tears in her eyes all during the ceremony, and she felt almost unbearably tense. She could not help noticing that the celebrant, Fr Sevron, was a good-looking young guy. He wasn't as handsome as her great heart-throb, the pop star David Essex, but he was the kind of bloke you wouldn't mind showing off to your girl-friends. Somehow the priest's youthful good looks only reminded her how she was physically repelled by the man she was marrying. She felt at that moment she would marry anyone other than her 'fiancé'.

Her intuition told her that the priest had come to sense during the ceremony that all was not well with this wedding, that maybe the bride did not really want to go ahead with it. He probably sensed that her tears were not tears of sentiment but of distress. Obviously the priest could not cancel the wedding just on a hunch. But Nuala got the impression that he was delaying the ceremony, going very slowly, so as to give her one last chance to back out. At one stage he said that he could not find the marriage rites. She heard him saying, 'I won't be a minute.' The thought came into her mind afterwards – was he giving her a chance to change her mind? It seemed to her that the Mass went on far longer than the average Mass. She was afraid her father was going to get up and say to the priest, 'Will you feckin' well marry her and get it over with!'

When Fr Sevron asked her if she took this man to be her lawful wedded husband, she could not bring herself to say 'I do'. The priest had to put the question three times. As she hesitated, she could feel the tension mounting in the church. Each time she was asked the vital question she turned around to look at her father in the front pew, this man who was forcing her into this loveless union. Each time he glared back at her, nodding at her, silently commanding her to say the words. Finally, she spoke the phrase that would seal her fate.

She was in shock for the entire day of her wedding. During the ceremony, she could not bear the idea of this man putting a ring on her finger. She grabbed the ring from him and put it on her finger herself. She did it out of defiance. Her attitude was that even though she was putting on this wedding ring, it certainly was not out of love.

In the weeks before the wedding, she often used to sit down with her mother and say, 'He will never go ahead with it. Never. What father would do this to his own daughter?' Even up to the morning that she was in her wedding dress, she still thought it was not going to happen. She would sob to her mother like a child, 'Will you come down there with me, Mammy? Will you stay with me in that house? It wouldn't be too bad if you came with me, Mammy. I can't stay there on my own with those two fellas, your man and the workman. Oh, it would be terrible. Please don't leave me alone there, Mammy.' Her mother would try to reassure her as best she could and say she would come with her, that she would visit her, that she would always be there for her.

Her mother would say, 'But you will have plenty of friends. You will never want for anything. You will have lovely clothes that your friends don't have, and other things that your friends won't have.' And Nuala would say to her, 'But I don't care, Mammy, I would rather be with my friends. I don't want to be different from all the other girls. None of them have boyfriends drawing the pension.' On the day of the wedding, before she got to the church, her mother tried to get her to look on the bright side, saying that she need not fear her father ever again. 'He will never rule you again, Nuala.'

After the ceremony, the wedding party went to a hotel and for the first time in her life Nuala smoked openly and drank alcohol. She had been stealing a drag from the odd cigarette, but never in front of her father. Now she felt it was time to rebel. She bought a packet of cigarettes and lit up ostentatiously in the hotel foyer, even though her father had always forbidden her to smoke. He himself remained a heavy smoker despite serious health problems – it was a case of do as I say, not as I do. She enjoyed a delicious moment of defiance when he strode over to her angrily and hissed at her, 'Take that cigarette out of your mouth or I'll kill you.' She replied cheekily, 'Daddy, I'm not your daughter any more. I'm a married woman now, and my husband tells me what to do. You can't order me around any more.' She enjoyed turning the tables on him. She reckoned that on the day in question, she'd get away with that small display of rebellion.

At the reception, she had a moment alone with the priest. Then she dropped her bombshell. Her tongue loosened by champagne, she told him, 'I did not want to marry this man at all. I was made to do it.' Fr Sevron was startled. If he had suspicions before, they were now borne out. He whispered to her urgently, 'But why didn't you tell me? You should have told me. Why didn't you even tell me at the altar?' Nuala's new husband was close by, and she couldn't say much else. The priest became very subdued and sombre. No doubt the enormity of the consequences for this teenager was dawning on him. Fr Sevron, who was to die at quite a young age, left the hotel shortly afterwards. Before he left, he came over to Nuala and shook hands with her. He told her he would pray for her. 'Thanks,' she said.

There were no speeches during the meal – a small mercy for which the bride was thankful. She was in no mood for sanctimonious clichés about the groom being welcomed into the family and other nonsense like that. Meanwhile, she got down to the serious business of getting drunk to blot out the memory of what had been done that day. The champagne was flowing and she knocked back glass after glass, until she was absolutely sloshed.

That evening, Nuala returned to her parents' house. The next day, she would move to Paddy's place. There was to be no honeymoon. There had been talk of a honeymoon, a tour of Killarney, but Nuala had put her foot down and refused to go. It was one of those rare occasions when she managed to get her way. Looking back now, she just cannot say how a honeymoon could have been squared with the prenuptial guarantee given to her that this would be a 'no sex' marriage. Would it have been a honeymoon with separate rooms, maybe even separate hotels? They would have been the oddest honeymoon couple in Killarney that year.

CHAPTER TWO

THE MATCH

When Nuala first saw the big, isolated country house, she felt uneasy. The Dickensian-style residence must once have been quite imposing, the proud home of a gentleman farmer. Now the rambling three-storey Georgian house with stables at the back had an air of faded elegance, and seemed to lack a woman's touch. With her teenager's attitude, Nuala felt that the house had a ghostly, eerie aura about it, and felt repelled.

It was a twist of fate that first brought Nuala and her father to the house. It was a fine day in late summer 1973, and sixteen-year-old Nuala was helping her fuel-merchant father make deliveries in a remote part of the country. Dan Slowney had some bags of anthracite coal in the back of a pick-up truck that he wanted to sell off and he decided to chance his luck by calling 'on spec' to the house surrounded by trees at the end of a long avenue.

As Dan steered his ramshackle truck up the long drive to the house, Nuala sat beside him in the passenger seat. Dan was puffing on a cigarette, his rough clothes and hands grubby from coal dust. All around were rolling green acres of good farmland. Cows grazed in the pastures, and the hedgerows and trees were in full bloom. The house might be a little unkempt, but there was still a good, big farm there. Dan cast a shrewd eye over the obvious affluence around him. If he smelled the fragrance of the fields through the open window of the truck on this bright summer's day, he gave no sign. Something far more interesting was assailing his nostrils – the smell of money.

He was fuming. The load of anthracite in the back of the truck had been intended for a local farming family, but they had decided that they did not really need it. This was mainly because, with his silver-tongued salesman's skills, Dan had talked them into buying a big load of coal just a few days previously. Then, in his greed, he tried to hit them again for more money by offering them another load. 'I do have the coal now, so better to buy it, because I may not have it later when it do get really cold, when yez will be freezing,' he told them. He delivered the second load, then had to listen to the two sisters in the house wittering on about how their brother was in bad health and how afraid they were that he might get a heart attack – and at the end of it all, after wasting his time, they decided that they did not need the extra fuel after all.

'I hope he does get the bloody heart attack,' murmured Dan as he drove along with Nuala beside him. It was more a question of talking out loud to himself rather than addressing his schoolgirl daughter. He never spoke to Nuala unless he had to, and she didn't say much to him unless she was spoken to. In Dan's macho world, real men didn't waste time on smalltalk with schoolgirls.

Dan was a determined salesman. He certainly did not plan to return home with the unwanted bags of fuel. Even though as a small-time merchant he had his own regular customers, he was going to call to a complete stranger to see if he could sell off the load. Dan didn't bother wasting his time on losers in labourers' cottages. He believed in going where the money was – and he sensed there was money in this big house.

Nuala looked glumly out the window as the pick-up rattled up the drive. She was a secret smoker and her nostrils longingly absorbed the aroma of her father's cigarette. She would have loved to ask him for a pull but he wasn't the type of father who would appreciate the request. He had forbidden his daughter to smoke and in their family his word was law. Smoking was fine for a man, but for a mere slip of a girl, well, that was a different story.

Nuala was on her summer holidays from the local convent secondary school. Like any other fun-loving teenage girl of that era, she loved pop music and reading girls' magazines, and often gazed longingly at the latest fashions in shop windows. The problem was, her father demanded that she work for him any chance she had. Her eldest brothers had flown the coop, and there were just a couple of other children at home, a boy and a girl. On that day, she certainly did not want to be delivering coal with her father. She wanted to be with her friends, doing the innocent things girls did, like talking about boyfriends or trying on her mother's lipstick. There was an aching resentment inside her that she was not allowed the freedoms that other girls had.

On this summer's day she was in her working clothes – jeans and a sweater – with her long hair tied up under a hat. She was tall, fit, strong – and very attractive. Dan was proud of his daughter's physical strength. It wasn't his style to pay compliments to the women in his family but he did, from time to time, give Nuala the ultimate accolade and assure her that she was really impressive at hauling sacks of coal and that, in this area at least, she was almost as good as any man.

It would have been nice to have got a compliment for her looks or her charm or her intelligence. But her ability to lift sacks of coal? Big deal! However, she knew better than to protest or give cheek to her father. She had an inclination towards impertinence, a trait she kept under control when her father was around. He didn't take kindly to impudence and she knew that if she stepped out of line the penalty would be a slap across the face. Helping her father deliver coal was certainly not the peak of her ambition, but her dad was the boss and she was used to giving him unquestioning obedience.

The elderly farmer was standing outside the house by the gracious limestone steps as the raucous rattle of the pick-up rang out amid the tranquillity of the fields. The house consisted of two storeys over a basement where the servants' quarters used to be. The man was attired in the usual farmer's garb of old trousers, the jacket of an old suit, check shirt, battered hat and wellington boots.

'Howaya boss,' said Dan, getting out of the truck.

'Not a bother,' said the farmer.

Dan, superb salesman that he was, quickly convinced the farmer that it was time to stock up on coal for the autumn, and duly made a sale. The farmer was a tall man, and he still looked fit despite his years. Nuala thought she detected a certain toughness or cruelty in his weatherbeaten features. Intuitively, she was wary of him. He had a workman with him, a middle-aged man called Sylvester, dressed in rough but clean working clothes, with a shiny forehead and a piercing stare. The thought of these two men in the eerie, isolated house made her feel even more uneasy. She wanted to get out of there as quickly as possible.

'Right,' Dan ordered with a satisfied grin, 'start unloading them bags.'

'Yes, Daddy.'

The elderly farmer looked with increasing interest at Nuala as she and Sylvester hefted the heavy bags of coal.

'Is that a boy or a girl?' the farmer asked Dan.

'It's a girl,' said Dan. 'It's my daughter.'

Somehow, Nuala guessed that Sylvester knew her gender all along and didn't have to ask that question. Sylvester was eyeing her up and down. She sensed that having established that she was a female, the farmer, Paddy McGorril, also began taking an extra degree of interest in her. What the hell was up with these guys? Hadn't they seen a girl before?

When the unloading was finished, the farmer invited Dan into the house. This hospitality was not extended to Nuala. She was just a girl, after all, and was thus excluded from 'man talk'. She sat back up in the passenger seat of the pick-up, waiting patiently for her father.

As Dan and the farmer finally emerged from the house after a con-siderable time, she noticed that her father was grinning. It was seldom she saw a smile on his face – only when he was making money, or conning some poor devil. She wondered what had been going on in the house.

The two men came over to Nuala. Dan gave her an instruction: 'Take off your hat and fix your hair.' Nuala obediently took off her hat and let her long hair fall down around her face and shoulders. Paddy seemed impressed.

'Oh, she's a girl all right,' he said as he stared at her.

Nuala sensed that the two men had been talking about her. She could smell whiskey off her father's breath – obviously the farmer's hospitality had been generous. Had they been celebrating? And if so, over what?

Nuala had her arm out the open window of the truck. And then a rather odd thing happened. Paddy began feeling the muscles in her arm and looking her up and down through the truck window.

She felt he was looking her over just as a farmer would size up cattle at a mart. She felt like a beast being inspected on a fair day. Her father looked on, still grinning. The workman was also looking at her, and she was looking warily at the workman. She said to herself, 'Jesus, this is a weird place.' She wondered if her father had got her a job working for the farmer – that's what was going through her mind. Was she going to become a farm labourer? She said to herself, 'I'm bloody well not coming in here to work in this weird place with these two characters.' She had a fear of men in general at the time, and she felt she couldn't get out of the place quickly enough.

She could hear snatches of an odd conversation between Paddy and her father, but the workman began to talk to her in his slow way, and she did not hear everything that was being said by the two other men. She heard the farmer saying to her father in his strong rural accent, 'She would be well looked after. She wouldn't want for anything. There would be no sex involved, nothing physical at all, at all. Just companionship, mind. She would be well off financially. She'd fall in for a lot whenever I pass on.' The farmer said that, with his wife dead a couple of years and his grown-up children moved away, he would like to have somebody for company. As they talked, the two men gave her sidelong glances. Obviously the farmer was looking for a wife.

Nuala's father, who was in his fifties, shook hands with the elderly farmer, and as he got into the truck he remarked casually to Nuala, 'See that man? He's going to be your husband.'

Nuala didn't take the remark seriously, and gave it little thought on the seven-mile journey home. No words were spoken on the drive along the quiet, narrow, leafy roads that cut through the lush green countryside and low hills in this tranquil part of rural Munster.

Dan's rundown cottage behind an unkempt hedge in the small hilltop village of Knockslattery was in stark contrast to the period residence they had just visited. In the field at the back of the house

Dan had some sheds where he stored the merchandise that he sold for a living – timber, turf, paling posts, some builders' supplies. He had a small sawmill at the back where he cut up firewood and sharpened the stakes used for fencing posts. The field was also where he parked his beat-up vehicles – the pick-up truck, two old cars that could barely splutter into life, and a decrepit old van. Parts of the field were overgrown with nettles and weeds, and at the back of the field there was a rat-infested stream. Dan usually kept animals on the land – a couple of pigs or a donkey or maybe a goat, and a few hens. Nearby, there were some local authority houses, a school, a post office and a shop. The village in those days had few signs of prosperity, and was not big enough to merit a church or a garda station. There were those who referred to Knockslattery unkindly as a 'one-horse town'.

Dan could have been well off from his business but he spent much of his money on drink and gambling. He used to have a small farm some distance away but that had been sold when Nuala was small. He would go off on drinking binges and the family might not see him for days. He was known in all the pubs where there was illegal afterhours drinking, and a knock on the window would be enough to get him in for a late-night drinking session. He could hold his drink. It would take an awful lot of pints for him to become drunk.

That evening Dan, his wife Josey, and Nuala gathered in the kitchen before the evening meal. Dan told his daughter to sit down. Then he announced, 'You're going to be a married woman soon.' Even then, she did not really take him seriously. But Josey was startled at this pronouncement.

'What do you mean, she's going to be a married woman soon?' she asked, an edge of anxiety in her voice.

'She's getting married to a grand chap. He do live beyond in Dunkellin. He have a big farm, a big house, plenty of cattle. He's a great catch. The wedding will be soon.'

'I can't believe this. Who exactly is this man?'

'Fella called Paddy McGorril. He have loads of money. Lovely fella. Widower. Nuala will fall in for everything when he dies. Sure the excitement of getting married to a young one will probably kill him off! We'll have the chance of a big farm, a big house.'

'How long have you known this man?'

'Met him today. Sold him a load of coal.'

'Oh God, Dan, what are you doing, for God's sake? What age is this man?'

'Mid-sixties, I'd say.'

'Ah now, Dan, for the love of Christ ...'

'But a young-looking mid-sixties. Doesn't look a day over fifty-five.'

Josey stood up from the table. 'Enough is enough. You can't do that to my daughter. I'm not having it. There's no way I'm going to allow it. You can't marry her off to a total stranger, and a man of his years, too. Ah, for God's sake, Dan, he's four times her age!'

Nuala was startled at her mother's outburst. Dan ruled his household with an iron hand. Both his wife and his children were in constant fear of him and his sudden bouts of violence. Josey Slowney was normally quiet and submissive. It would take a lot for her to openly defy Dan like she had just done. Maybe her mother sensed something that Nuala herself didn't. Nuala had been wondering if she should really take her father's crazy proposition seriously. Surely he had to be joking, she had thought. But her mother's reaction was ominous, and made her think again.

Dan got up from the table and silenced his wife's protests with a glare. He didn't have to raise his hand or make a verbal threat – his body language spoke volumes. A deeply upset Josey busied herself silently around the kitchen, preparing the evening meal. Nuala picked up all the signs. Even though violence at home, or the threat of violence, was nothing new to her, she never got used to it.

Nuala began to sob as she heard the plans for her future life unfold. 'Daddy, there's no way I am marrying that old man. I don't want to live in that big house with him and the other fella.' She was worried too about what her friends would say. She didn't want to be embarrassed in front of them. And she was thinking of the big, eerie house and the two men living there, and her having to live there with them. The thought sent shivers down her spine.

Dan looked at Nuala and said, 'You're marrying him, and that's it.'

Nuala's eighteen-year-old brother Conor and her twelve-year-old sister Fidelma came in for tea. Fidelma chattered away as the family sat down for the evening meal but she soon stopped talking as she noticed the heavy silence. Josey was subdued as she served up the boiled eggs, poured the tea and buttered the bread. Dan disappeared off to the pub after the meal, and Nuala helped her mother do the washing up. The atmosphere lightened a little.

Conor, who had been taken out of school to work with his father, began to pull Nuala's leg in the kitchen, saying, 'Nuala's getting married.'

Nuala swung around from the sink and glared at him. 'Shut up, you,' she said.

Fidelma got excited. 'Are you really getting married, Nuala? Oh that's great. Weddings are great. They give you this lovely cake and there's always loads of lemonade. When is it going to be? Is it Larry you're marrying?'

'No, it's not,' grinned Conor. 'It's some other fella with loads and loads of money. I heard Daddy saying it.'

'Oh who is he, Nuala?' said Fidelma. 'Is he nice? Ah go on, tell us.'

'Now stop this,' said Josey. 'Nuala is not getting married to anybody, not to Larry or anybody else. She is staying at school to do her Leaving Cert, and will then be getting a good job.'

'But I thought I heard Daddy saying –' said Conor.

'That's enough now,' said Josey.

As they all settled in to watch TV, Nuala said to her brooding mother, 'Mammy, I'm going to the shop for crisps. Then I'm calling around to see Carmel.'

Nuala badly wanted somebody to talk to. There was no point in turning to the two siblings who were still at home, Conor and Fidelma. She felt she had little personal rapport with them. Conor was the deep, silent type who didn't say much at the best of times, and Fidelma was several years younger than Nuala and still only a child. She knew that her best friend Carmel would provide a ready ear to her troubles. Carmel was a girl her own age who was at the same convent school, and who lived a few minutes' walk away.

'What's the *craic*, Nuala?' Carmel was always in a good mood. Whenever she talked, there always seemed to be an air of suppressed laughter underneath. How she managed to be so upbeat all the time, Nuala could not figure out. Apart from being her best pal, Nuala liked her because she always cheered her up. Carmel could be cheeky and outspoken, and she got away with saying things that others would be scared to say. They went for a walk along the main street, and out into the country, sharing the bag of crisps that Nuala had bought, and chattering away, as teenagers do. There were few cars on the move to shatter the sense of calm that lay over the green fields on either side of the narrow, potholed tarmacadam road.

'How's Larry?' asked Carmel.

'He's busy on the farm. He won't be calling around for a few nights.'

'I always know when he's at your house. It's hard to miss that huge big car. It's almost like the ones that politicians swan around in.'

'Do you see that, Carmel?' said Nuala, holding out her thumb. 'I have him firmly under that.' They both laughed.

'Fair play to you, Nuala. I wouldn't mind going out with him me-self.'

'Did you buy the latest *Smash Hits*?'

'Yeah. Do you want me to keep it for you?'

'Would you mind? I'm skint at the moment. Oh Jaysus, I'm knackered from delivering coal, and the da never thinks of putting his hand in his pocket to give me a few bob. I'm still only on pocket money.'

'Don't tell me your oul' fella still has you working on the coal? Why don't you tell him to piss off? Imagine having coal delivery on your c.v. if you're going for some posh office job in Dublin.'

'The older lads are in England now, and it's all falling on me and Conor.'

'Will we stroll down to the creamery gates?' said Carmel. 'There's going to be a crowd down there tonight. We'll have a bit of fun.'

'I have to be back home soon. Let's just talk for a while. There's a couple of things I want to tell you.'

'Sure.'

Nuala paused for a moment. 'You'll never guess what Daddy's latest stunt is,' she said at last.

'Let me try. He's going to open a pub, with himself as the best customer. Or maybe it's a bookie's shop – again with himself as the best customer.'

'He wants me to marry this old farmer we met today delivering coal.'

'Ah you're making this up.'

'I swear I'm not. Cross my heart.'

'Who is he?'

'Some old geezer over in Dunkellin. He's ancient. I can't even re-member his bloody name. Gives me the creeps.'

'Was your dad pissed out of his mind when he said it?'

'He did have a few on him.'

'Well there, that explains it. It's the beer talking as usual. Not even *your* father would do that to his own daughter.'

'You're probably right.'

'You know something? Your oul' lad really talks a load of shite, doesn't he?'

They laughed, but Nuala still felt a nagging sense of unease.

CHAPTER THREE

THE SELLER OF DREAMS

He walked into the kitchen in a slow, ponderous way, with the exaggerated dignity of someone seriously drunk. It was tea time, and Josey was serving toast and scrambled eggs at the kitchen table. The glint in Dan's eye as he surveyed the scene was enough to silence the chatter around the table. They had seen that look before. The fire had gone down a little. Dan stared at it and then at Josey. A look of disbelief came over his face. He shook his head, as if he could not fathom how any woman could let a fire die down like that. He was annoyed and didn't care who knew it.

'Were you off with a man all day, you fucking whore?' he roared, the words slurred from the effects of the alcohol. Josey was trembling, her voice on the edge of tears, saying, 'Sure I have everything done, the place is spotless ...' To show the depth of his hurt and annoyance at Josey's neglect of her household duties, Dan grabbed the table and up-ended it. Nuala felt a stab of pain. Her chin was cut by the edge of the table as it overturned with a crash. She was only about five at the time. The children scattered, screaming with shock and terror. Crockery was smashed, and the remains of the modest meal ended up in a mess on the floor.

Then Dan closed in on the woman who had just caused him such serious offence. He grabbed his wife and began to rain blows and slaps down on her. He would teach her to let the fire go down. He would teach her to neglect the house. She was roaring and crying and pleading with him to stop and the children were all shouting through their tears, 'Daddy, don't, please don't hit Mammy.'

Josey managed to escape his grip and ran out into the back garden. The children ran out to see where she was. She had jumped into a clump of nettles, and was cowering in the undergrowth being stung by them. Nuala saw the terror on the face of her mother. Nuala's eldest brother Malachy was fifteen, and very tall. He had had enough. He caught his father and hit him, and flung him onto the floor of the kitchen. Dan lay there, bleeding and shocked. The boy picked up a hatchet and stood over him and said, 'If you don't leave my mother alone I will fucking kill you.' Dan was suddenly silent. Just as suddenly as it had flared up, his aggression drained away. His rampage was over and he never retaliated. Maybe bullies get a shock when somebody stands up to them. A couple of days later Malachy ran away from home in disgust and went to England. He didn't come back to visit for almost thirteen years.

The fact that one of his sons had threatened to kill him did not deter Dan from further outbreaks of drunken violence. As a child, Nuala dreaded the nights her father would come home drunk and wake up herself and the other kids and drag them up out of their beds. They knew what they were going to witness. They were going to see their mother being kicked and beaten. There were times when Dan didn't regard it as sufficient to thrash his terrified wife in private – he preferred to do it before an audience of his weeping children. It was one of the ways in which he showed off his power within his own household.

And now, the total power that he wielded in his family circle was one of the reasons why Josey was helpless to do anything effective to save her daughter as Dan began the process of marrying her off to an elderly stranger. Josey had been terrorised for much of her married life, and the beatings she took from her husband are still etched in Nuala's memory. On one occasion, he knocked out Josey's teeth. Another time, he left her in hospital with an injured hip. In her mind's eye, Nuala can still see her mother hunched up on the floor like a frightened animal and this man beating her. Nuala never loved her father. How could anyone love a man who would behave like that?

One night, despite being extremely drunk, Dan dreamed up an exquisite mental torture for Josey. She loved delph, and had it neatly arrayed on a dresser. Dan grinned as he grabbed the dresser. Josey could see what was going to happen. Dan's grin grew broader as she pleaded with him, 'Oh Jesus, Mary and Joseph, please don't.' He paused for a few more moments. And then, with one heave, he sent dresser and crockery all crashing to the floor. The smashing of the crockery was just a starter, with the main course consisting of a savage beating. Josey could take no more and she took drastic action. She fled the house and took refuge with a relative.

When he sobered up, Dan was dumbfounded and, amazingly, contrite. He hadn't reckoned on her actually walking out. How was he to cope on his own? How was he to look after the children? Who was to do the cooking and the washing up? He was obsessed with the idea of a good fire in the grate, and who would keep that going? He got all the kids to dress up in their Sunday best, loaded them into the back of his pick-up truck, drove off to a nearby town, bought a load of crockery to replace what he had smashed, and then proceeded in the truck with kids, delph and all, to the house where his wife was staying. His apologies were most abject, and he swore he would never drink again. His wife, obviously moved by this rare show of remorse and Dan's elaborate promises of better behaviour in the future, consented to return home, and she climbed into the cabin of the truck.

On the way home Dan stopped at a pub. Josey was aghast. She said to him, 'Ah Dan, I thought you said ...' He gave her a sly grin and replied, 'Sure it's just the one.' He brought them all into the bar, and they had lemonade while he knocked back several pints – despite his promises that he would never touch a drop ever again. Nuala felt, even as a child, that this was typical of him. She could never really believe a word out of his mouth.

Apart from his drinking and his violence, Nuala had another reason to hate her father. Dan had a murky secret – he had molested Nuala for about two years from the age of nine. He would creep into her bedroom at night, take off her nightdress and fondle her, trying to convince her that he was simply showing her affection. She didn't believe him. She hated and feared these sessions and despised him for what he was doing to her.

'Don't tell anybody about this. It's our little secret, right?' he would say.

She became so upset she said to him, 'I'm telling my Mammy. I'm telling my Mammy.'

Dan stopped creeping into her room after that. Nuala believes it was because he was afraid she would blow the gaff on him. But somehow the fact that he could use her at his whim just reinforced the sense of power that hung around him.

Drink was a dominant theme in Dan's life. Even trips to Sunday Mass with the family gave him the chance to slip away to the pub. Dan always brought the family to Mass on Sundays. He would march down the aisle, himself in the lead with Josey and the children following close behind. Then he would slip out of the church and head off to the pub, and when the Mass was over he would drive them all home again. While he never seemed to bother to go to the sacraments, he did pray the rosary with the family from time to time – whenever he happened to be stuck at home because he didn't have the money to go out drinking. Nuala remembers him getting up off his knees after the rosary once and hitting Josey because the fire had died down. The fire was always an excuse for him to throw his weight around.

Josey was very religious. She never lost the faith and prayed a lot. She had a bleak, difficult life. Apart from Sunday Mass, one of the big moments of her week was to watch *The Late Late Show* on TV. It was on a Saturday night in those days. Dan would only look at it if he was short of the money to go to the pub. Josey idolised the *Late Late* host Gay Byrne. She thought he was one of the most handsome men she had ever seen. The other TV highlight of the week for Josey and the kids was *The Fugitive*, a drama series about a doctor on the run after being accused of murdering his wife. 'Oh I hope he gets away,' Josey would pray as each cliffhanger episode came to a close. 'The poor fella. They're always chasing him; and I wouldn't mind but he's innocent, he never killed her.'

It wasn't just the drink that turned Dan violent. He could also turn vicious if he lost at gambling. He was a great supporter of Gaelic games, and would never miss a match. He would attend football and hurling matches or watch them on TV in the pub or in a friend's house. Often he would gamble on the outcome. Josey would know he had gambled on the county team to win, and she would be at home on tenterhooks watching the game on TV, hoping against hope that the home side would taste victory, and that Dan would win money, be in good humour, and not beat her up.

If his team won, he would come in drunk after the pubs closed, singing the same song over and over, 'I'll Take You Home Again

Kathleen', and Josey and the children would know he had won money and they would breathe a sigh of relief. If the team lost, they would hear him slamming the car door in resentment and they would know then that they were in for it. Josey would have been watching the match on television herself, praying at the screen, 'Oh let them win, let them get a point or a goal, for God's sake!' Nuala used to resent the way their fate depended on the outcome of a game – 'all that worry and misery and brutality, and all over a stupid match'.

Dan would stake anything on a gamble. Nuala loved animals, and was delighted with one of the few presents her father ever gave her – an elderly donkey. She adored the decrepit animal, and took loving care of it. One Monday morning she was distraught and almost frantic with worry to find that the donkey had disappeared. It later emerged that the previous day her father had gambled on the outcome of a hurling match. He had no money, so he put up the donkey as a stake against a cash wager from a friend. Dan lost the bet, so Nuala's beloved pet was hustled away in the dead of night in settlement of the wager. Nuala was about twelve at the time. She never saw the donkey again. She cried her eyes out. Her father didn't care what he gambled away.

Dan didn't give a damn about rules or laws that didn't suit him. Driving while drunk was part of his regular routine. Getting into a vehicle with him meant taking your life in your hands. Nuala travelled with him on a few occasions in the pick-up truck when he was absolutely stocious, the vehicle weaving perilously from side to side of the road. She thought it was a miracle that he never mowed down one of the neighbours or had a fatal encounter with a wall or an electricity pole. Dan did have crashes and, unfortunately from her point of view, survived them. He came home a few times with gashes in his head, but the injuries were never serious enough for him to go to hospital. She would think sometimes of all the decent people who died in road accidents and how a monster like him did all the wrong things and still survived. Her mother used to say that the devil is where the drink is, and that it was the devil that always brought him home safely.

Almost as if he were a Jekyll and Hyde character, Dan could be enormously cruel at home but full of charm to those whom he encountered in the pub or on his rounds as a fuel merchant. And it was that charm that helped him to dabble in a sideline as a matchmaker, a job that required much skill in dealing with people and their sensitivities. Matchmaking was an activity that had flourished in generations past in rural Ireland but by the middle of the twentieth century had largely died out. Dan was one of the rare specimens of his 'profession' to survive. Few outside his own community knew of his sideline. He never sought or received publicity. Even into the 1960s and early 1970s, there were those who discreetly sought out his skills. If a man or woman had difficulty finding a spouse, the matchmaker would be brought in as an intermediary to bridge the gap. The matchmaker was a one-man rural version of the modern marriage bureau. He didn't have an office, shunned the telephone and never advertised. He was known through word of mouth and never kept accounts or records. Deals were done over a bottle of whiskey in the kitchen of a farmhouse or the back room of a pub.

Dan was ideally placed to make matches – his work delivering fuel took him to houses in many parts of the countryside; he had a wide circle of contacts and knew the farmers who were hungering for a wife and the women who were pining for a man. He was the kind of wheeler-dealer who could sell an old bachelor farmer a load of coal, and fix him up with a woman at the same time. Admittedly, it might not be a woman in the first flush of youth. She might not be a ravishing beauty. But at least the farmer had got himself a wife to share his twilight years. Dan's shrewd eye could detect when a 'prospect' was ripe for the picking. He could tell when an elderly bachelor was desperate to experience even a little wedded bliss before he passed away, and he could tell when a spinster desperately wanted to tie the knot and have a baby before the biological clock stopped ticking forever. The loneliness, the frustration, the desperation, the great hunger for sexual fulfilment that often lay below the seemingly placid surface of Irish rural life in former times all combined to provide him with clients.

Dan's outgoing personality no doubt helped to enhance his reputation as a matchmaker. He could be soft and generous to people outside the family. If a drinking buddy asked him for a loan of money, he got it, no bother. He was a great storyteller, and was generous in the pub, buying round after round of drinks. So many people loved him, considering him a real gent. All these qualities helped to enhance Dan's abilities as a salesman, and salesmanship was one of the necessary qualities of a matchmaker. After all, he was 'selling' some of the most fundamental things in human life – love, romance, sex, marriage, procreation. In effect, he was a seller of dreams.

His motivation as a matchmaker was money. Mostly the fees were modest, but from time to time there was the chance to make a big profit. His antennae were always active; he was ever on the alert for the lucrative deal, for the big killing. His attitude was, 'There's money in marriages.'

In addition to selling fuel and paling posts and arranging matches,

Dan had another sideline – antiques. Anything there was money to be made from, Dan was in on it. He was always on the make. If he went into a house and saw a fine piece of furniture, he would say to the person, 'There's woodworm in that oul' thing. I'll take it off your hands and there'll be a nice few bob in it for you.' Dan knew a dealer and anything he bought on his rounds he would sell on to this dealer. He was like a rural Irish version of Arthur Daly, the wheeler dealer character in the British TV series *Minder*.

As a matchmaker, Dan would follow a certain ritual. First he would bring the man along to meet the woman. This would mostly happen in a pub, maybe in the back room. If they liked each other, if they clicked and it looked like a marriage was on the cards, there would be £50 put on the table – £25 from each person, if their financial backgrounds were similar. This money would be given to a trusted third party to hold, usually the publican. There would be a drinking session that night to celebrate the match. The couple would start courting and, if the wedding took place, the matchmaker was given the £50 on the day of the ceremony, minus a cut for the person who had held the money. Dan would be invited to the wedding. For him it would be a great day out, as he could expect to be plied with free drink all day.

Nuala and the other children were not supposed to know about the matchmaking. Dan would not talk to them about it, although Nuala remembers as a child her father leaving the house and saying to her mother, 'I'm going out matchmaking.' She learned later from other people how it worked. Her father would approach a woman who was looking for a husband and say to her, 'I know a man, he have a few pound, he's a lovely man, would you like to meet him?' There was one poor woman and he was always bringing men to see her but they

THE SELLER OF DREAMS

never clicked. Often the woman would have to have money of her own to bring to the marriage, but some farmers would take a woman with no money, and in some cases the farmer would put up the entire £50 fee for the matchmaker.

In certain cases a farmer might not only take a woman with no money, but pay a huge fee to the matchmaker for fixing him up with a girl who was young and attractive. In a case like this, it wasn't just a question of a £50 fee – the payment could run into thousands. There were a lot of middle-aged and elderly bachelor farmers around. Many of them were men who had waited for years to inherit the family farm before deciding to get married, and then it was very hard for them to find a wife, and as they got older they became more desperate. Many of them would be looking for a woman young enough to give them an heir, and if she was attractive as well that would be the icing on the cake. But there were always those thrifty-minded farmers who, while they might prefer an attractive young woman, would settle for an older, plainer one if she had a bit of land.

Many years after it took place a woman friend confided to Nuala that a match had been arranged for her. Her father was an acquaintance of Dan's and with his approval Dan introduced a wealthy old farmer to her. Because she was relatively young and reasonably attractive, it was reckoned that Dan could have pocketed well over £1,000 from the farmer for fixing him up with her. The downside in this case was that the young woman was an alcoholic who could drink like a fish. The cost of keeping her in booze would have been considerable. But Dan made sure that the toothless old farmer was carefully kept in the dark as regards this blemish in his would-be bride, and the lovestruck pensioner was champing at the bit to wed her. The attraction of the deal for the young woman would be that, with any luck, the farmer would die off quickly and she would get her hands on a good farm. She might then be able to marry again, this time for love instead of land. In the end, the woman backed out. She told Nuala many years on, 'I just couldn't do it, Nuala. I couldn't wake up beside that thing in the morning, drunk or sober.'

Because of his background as a matchmaker, Dan was well-placed to make a match between his daughter and Paddy. However, this match was very different from anything that had gone before. The other matches were done on a voluntary basis with two mature people agreeing of their own free will to consider marriage and perhaps ultimately to tie the knot. On this occasion, the bride-to-be was just a schoolgirl, the matchmaker's own daughter, and the match was being arranged without her consent. She was to be fixed up with a man who could never, in a million years, get her to love him.

CHAPTER FOUR

THE COURTSHIP

A few days after Nuala broke the news of the marriage plans to Carmel, they were out walking again. It was a fine, tranquil evening in Knockslattery. A small group of youths had gathered in their usual spot near the village shop. Their shouts and the sounds of their horseplay echoed along the main street. The lads were in a cheeky, irreverent mood and the two girls crossed the street to avoid them.

'Was it love at first sight?' one of the youths called out as his pals sniggered.

Nuala blushed. The insult cut through her like a knife.

'Oh God,' she murmured. 'If they know, everybody knows.'

'Leave this to me,' said Carmel.

Looking tough in her bomber jacket and jeans, Carmel strode across the street to the group of boys, her shoulders thrown back with aggression. They kept grinning but Carmel could see the apprehension in their eyes. They hadn't expected anybody to confront them.

Carmel poked her nose into the face of the leering sixteen-year-old who had made the remark.

'Billy, if you say anything like that again, do you know what I will do?'

'What?'

'I will break your fuckin' face.'

Nuala and Carmel went on with their walk and when they were quite some distance away they could hear one of the youths calling out, to the laughter of his mates, 'How's the sugar-daddy?'

Nuala shuddered. 'I wonder how they found out.'

'Ah they're only little gougers – don't mind them.'

As the days passed, Nuala still could not take seriously the prepos-terous idea of getting married to this elderly farmer. Cynical and all as her father was, surely he would not force her into a marriage with a total stranger four times her age? How could even a pervert inflict such a horror on his own daughter? She didn't mind people getting married with a big age gap between them. She wasn't a bigot about it. Sometimes a young woman fell in love with a much older man, or an older woman might go for a very young lad. The best of luck to them was her attitude. What was the problem if that was what they wanted? What she hated was that nobody was giving her a choice. Her spirits fell as the signs began to accumulate that her father was in deadly earnest about the 'match'.

One of the first things Dan decided was that Nuala's long hair would have to go. Nuala had always gloried in the beautiful tresses that fell down around her shoulders. People would admire her lovely hair, but her father reckoned it only emphasised her tender years. He wanted her to look older so that the vast gap in age between herself and her 'fiancé' would appear less obvious. So Dan called in a woman neighbour who put a towel around Nuala's shoulders and proceeded to crop her hair.

Despite the shadow hanging over her future, Nuala tried to get on with her life as best she could. She already had a boyfriend, Larry, but she wasn't in love with him and didn't see him all the time. With typical teenage fantasy, the person she was really in love with was somebody she had never even met – the singer David Essex.

One evening around this time her brother Conor came into the kitchen after tea and said, 'Nuala, look at this.'

Nuala gasped. She almost went weak at the knees. Her brother was unfolding an almost life-size poster of David Essex. It was bigger and better than any of the posters of the pop idol that she had collected before.

A childish bartering ensued.

'Where did you get that?'

'You know my pal Liam? Well, his sister got it out of a magazine, and she didn't want it.'

'I have to have it,' said Nuala immediately. 'I just have to have it. What do you want for it?'

'You know those two toffee bars that you have hidden away in your room? Well, I want them bars, and two bags of crisps.'

'Feck's sake, Conor, how did you know about the bars?'

He gave her a sly grin. 'Is it a deal?'

'How about two toffee bars and just one bag of crisps?'

'What kind of crisps?'

'Cheese and Onion.'

'Okay. Done.'

Nuala proudly added another David Essex poster to her collection. She thought, just wait until Carmel sees it – she'll be mad jealous. Apart from the posters, she had two precious David Essex records – singles that she had obtained by bartering sweets and magazines with her friends. All she had to play them on was an ancient wind-up gramophone which some elderly client had given to Dan in part payment for a load of anthracite. It was really more a piece of furniture than a gramophone. The scratchy sound was awful, like the sound of an early John McCormack record, but it was better than nothing.

Conor was not just her brother, these days he was also her chaperone.

If any semi-serious young boyfriend came along, he had to take on not only Nuala but Conor too. They came as a package. Dan didn't like the idea of young men going out with his daughter without supervision, so Conor would be instructed to tag along when they went out on a date. Conor didn't mind going – it was something to do.

Nuala's boyfriend Larry was a farmer in his twenties, and the son of a prosperous farmer. Larry was a courteous young man who treated her well and Nuala liked him. But she did not take the relationship seriously, even though he was mad about her and wanted to marry her. She had been going out with Larry for about a year. He thought she was older than she really was. They had met at a local barn dance in aid of some parish project. It was the kind of country dance that everyone attended, young and old.

Nuala and her younger sister Fidelma were the hit of the evening, as they gave a dazzling display of jiving. Couples moved out of their way to give them space as the band belted out some old Elvis Presley rock-'n'-roll numbers. The two girls loved to dance, and it was reckoned there were no better rock-'n'-rollers in Knockslattery. The band, consisting of a few local guys with accordions, guitars and fiddles, also played 'The Walls of Limerick' and 'The Siege of Ennis', and the older people took the floor with whoops of delight for these fast-moving traditional Irish dances.

When an old-time waltz was announced, Larry asked Nuala's father if he could dance with her. Dan and Josey and their children were standing in a corner of the hall. Dan, through his top-class local intelligence network, knew Larry's background and instantly decided he might be a good prospect. He gave the go-ahead to the young farmer to take to the floor with his daughter. Dan approved of Larry because he was going to inherit a big farm and he drove a Mercedes. Larry, who often visited Nuala at home after that, remained in favour because he would bring Dan out drinking and Larry would often insist on buying. There were times when Dan, as the saying went, didn't have to put his hand in his pocket. He thought Larry was 'a lovely fella'.

The relationship between Larry and Nuala was a very innocent one, never going beyond holding hands. He would bring her to the pictures and to dances and also to the pub, although she would only drink lemonade. Conor, of course, would go along on all these outings. He would sit in the front of the car with Larry, while Nuala sat in the back. In the cinema or the pub, Nuala would sit in the middle, Larry on one side and Conor on the other. Conor didn't mind chaperone duty as he got to go on plenty of outings, with Larry footing the bill. Going to the cinema in one of the big towns in the region, Nuala could have anything she wanted to eat – crisps, chocolate, ice cream or popcorn. And whatever she got, Conor got the same. It was great fun for him, and since Larry was a real gent, he didn't have much to do in terms of chaperone duty. Conor never talked much, and so didn't get in the way of conversations between Nuala and Larry, although he would hear almost everything that was said.

The three of them went to see *Ryan's Daughter* a total of four times. Larry had a grand-aunt who was in the movie, which had been made in County Kerry. Admittedly she was only an extra, who appeared fleetingly in one crowd scene wearing a shawl. She had no speaking lines. But for Larry the highlight of the evening was when her image flickered briefly onto the screen – her two seconds of fame. Larry and Nuala and Conor would be on the lookout for her and each time they went to see the film Larry would point her out proudly. 'That's her there,' he would say. 'Did you see her?

That's Aunt Nellie.'

There were country dance halls within driving distance that they also visited. The trio danced to the music of some of the big show-bands of the era: The Indians, Daddy Cool and the Lollipops, and Big Tom and the Mainliners. Larry would dance with Nuala, and Conor would have the occasional dance with her as well. Conor would also dance with other girls his own age, some of whom he knew. And when the dance was over there would be another treat in store. Larry would bring them to a takeaway for chips – and sometimes he would even throw in three portions of chicken to go with the chips.

Larry used to buy presents for Nuala, sometimes expensive things such as a watch. When Larry would call around to the house, Dan would give Nuala a wink as if to say, 'Get as much as you can out of him.' Larry told Dan in the pub one night that he would like to marry Nuala. Dan said, 'Of course you can.' Marriage was the furthest thing from Nuala's mind, although, had she been older and a little more mature, she reckons now she might have agreed to become his wife.

As soon as old Paddy McGorril came on the scene, Larry got short shrift from Dan. It was anybody's guess when Larry would actually inherit the farm, so any major dividends from a marriage to Nuala could be far in the future. In contrast, Paddy was seen by Dan as a far superior prospect – he already had a good farm of land, was advanced in years and, with the help of God, might not live that long. So it was a question of 'goodbye, Larry'. All Larry's generosity, the outings to the pubs, the buying of pints for Dan, the presents to Nuala, all this largesse was suddenly forgotten. Dan's orders to Nuala were laconic and very much to the point: 'Get rid of him. Next time he calls, bring him into the back garden and tell him you can't see him again.'

Nuala felt awful about this. She felt she was being made to do her father's dirty work. If Dan wanted rid of Larry, why couldn't he do it himself? She felt it was terrible to be giving Larry the bum's rush after he had become such a family friend. By now Larry was a close drinking buddy of Dan's and yet he was to be told he was no longer welcome as the boyfriend of Dan's daughter. She felt so embarrassed. But she didn't feel like arguing with her father either. Dan had spoken. The case was closed.

The next night that Larry called around to the house, Nuala asked him to go with her into the back garden as she had something to tell him. Then, with all the brutal directness of youth, she gave it to him straight. 'I can't see you again. I'm getting married to somebody else. You're not to call around any more.'

Larry was speechless for a moment. He looked as if he had been kicked in the stomach. 'What? What are you telling me? I don't understand.'

'I'm getting married to a farmer. He's an oul' lad. I don't want to marry him. I hate him but Daddy is making me do it.'

Larry was aghast. 'I can't believe this is happening.'

They talked for a while. She told him about the man she was supposed to be marrying and how she just did not want to go ahead with the match.

Nuala began grasping at straws and said to Larry, 'I don't suppose there's any chance that you could marry me?' She knew almost immediately it was the wrong thing to say. She would obviously just be using Larry as an escape route.

He told her, 'Nuala, I can't marry you like that. You have to marry out of love. I love you but I don't think that you really love me. If you don't marry me out of love it's no good.'

'Ah, to hell with love. I can come to love you, can't I?' she replied. Looking back on it now, she realises she didn't know at the time what love meant at all.

They talked some more. Larry was heartbroken. There wasn't much more he could say. Then Nuala took a ring he had given her off her finger and handed it back to him.

'No, Nuala, you keep it,' he said.

They shook hands, and her crestfallen former sweetheart walked glumly out of the garden, and out of her life forever.

When Nuala came back into the house, Dan said to her, 'Is he gone?'

'Yes, Daddy.'

'Good girl.'

With Larry safely dumped, the 'romance' between Nuala and Paddy got under way. This time, there would be no need for Conor as a 'minder' – Larry's departure had made Conor redundant as the family chaperone. Dan gave a kick-start to the courtship by taking Nuala and her mother to Paddy's house on a visit. This was the first time that Nuala had seen Paddy since their initial bizarre encounter a few days previously. Again, Paddy looked Nuala up and down, sizing her up, but he never said anything to her. He talked to her father and made arrangements and plans, but nobody actually addressed her. Paddy went on about what he could give her, the house and the farm, and the life that she would have. Neither he nor her father ever thought of asking her what she wanted.

She looked at the house and farm with the mind of a child. A great animal-lover, she struck up an immediate rapport with Lassie, the black-and-white sheepdog. Among the visitors, Lassie seemed to single her out for a special welcome. Nuala patted Lassie and talked to the dog, who whimpered with delight and licked her hand. The two took an immediate liking to each other. Nuala knew she would love to see Lassie again. Also, Nuala was a tomboy who loved climbing trees, and she thought there would be great climbing in some of the trees around the house. But she still could not believe she would ever actually live there. She was wary of Paddy partly because, to her, he had a vicious appearance. She later saw a photo of him when he was young, and he was very handsome. But even as a young man he looked hard.

Paddy laid on supper for his guests. There were sweets, cakes, biscuits and sandwiches laid out on the big mahogany table in the dining room. After a wink and a nod from her father, Nuala slipped a few of the delicacies into her pocket to bring home to Conor and Fidelma. They were thrilled.

'Oh Nuala,' said Fidelma, 'will you keep going to that fella's house, will you? Please? Will you bring us home more sweets?'

Nuala's aged 'fiancé' began calling around to her own home. She cringed as he arrived for the first time. Looking out a window, she saw the car drawing up outside and this elderly man in his Sunday suit and a hat with a feather on it being welcomed like a celebrity by her father, who could really turn on the charm when he got the smell of easy money. The visitor would never talk to her in any meaningful way. He would just sit there looking at her. Occasionally he would ask her how she was getting on at school. When he did say something to her it was as if he was talking to a child. He would mostly talk to her father or her mother. She was usually the topic of conversation. She would only speak when told to speak. Her father would say to her before he arrived, 'Be nice to him now, and take that surly look off your face. Put on a smile.' He would ask her father what were her favourite biscuits and sweets, and her father would have her primed to look for the most expensive if she were ever asked. She and the other kids would not be getting these delicacies at home. Before that, she was lucky if she got a penny toffee.

Dan wanted to convince Paddy that in marrying Nuala he was getting a paragon of housewifely virtue. Dan would arrange for the ironing to pile up, and the sound of Paddy's car arriving would be the cue for Nuala to get stuck into the ironing with single-minded gusto. Or she would be put to polishing the floor like mad on her knees as Paddy came up to the front door. As Nuala slaved away, Dan would lounge back in his chair and casually make pointed remarks to Paddy, like, 'Isn't that a great young one there – she can do anything around the house.'

A couple of times Paddy asked her to come with him out to his car when he was leaving her parents' house. She was repelled by the idea of being alone with Paddy in a 'romantic' situation, but she felt she had no choice. She had nothing to say to this man who was old enough to be her grandfather and who seemed like he belonged to a different century. On one occasion he gave her a locket and said, 'When we marry your photo will be in that.' She said 'Thanks' and thought to herself, 'That'll be the day!' He gave her a peck on the cheek and she pulled away from him. She shuddered with disgust. She spent ages washing her face afterwards with carbolic soap. She had to wear the locket whenever he would come around. In the end, she gave the locket to her mother, telling her she didn't want it.

Paddy began taking Nuala and her parents to hotels for meals. Eating out was something she was not used to, and there was a certain novelty about these lunches. Paddy still didn't talk much to Nuala, except to say, 'You will never want for anything. You will always have lovely things. You will never have to do anything.' She was not impressed. Her father would knock back the drinks during the meal, with Paddy footing the bill. Before the outing, Dan would warn his daughter on what to say and what not to say. 'Just say what you're supposed to say,' Dan would tell her. On one occasion, when she had a few moments alone with Paddy, she plucked up the courage to speak her mind.

'You know, I am not marrying you,' she said, with all the defiance she could muster.

A very disgruntled Paddy told her father what she had said.

That evening Dan called his daughter into the kitchen. He began the 'conversation' by slapping her across the face.

'How dare you say you are not marrying him.' He slapped her again. And again. 'You're marrying him and that's the end of it.'

One evening at home, Nuala summoned up the courage to say to her father, 'Daddy, I'll run away from home rather than marry him.' She was afraid he might hit her but, speaking very calmly, he just threatened her. 'If you try to run away, I'll catch you, and when I catch you, you will be in for it.'

Then she watched as he went out to one of the sheds in the back and came in with a hammer and some long nails. He went into her bedroom and nailed down the window so that she could not open it and make her getaway. The message was clear – her home was to become like a jail. The window looked out onto the sheds at the back of the house. She began to be kept under constant supervision, becoming a virtual prisoner in her own home. She was furious with herself. Why had she opened her big mouth anyway about wanting to escape? If she had been really clever she would have pretended to go along with the marriage, and then have done a runner when Dan least expected it.

When Dan had to go away from home he would lock Nuala into her bedroom, using a padlock to secure the latch. His orders were that she was only to be allowed out to go to the toilet and that her meals were to be handed in to her. Her mother would let her out of the bedroom when the coast was clear. But the front door would also be secured with a deadlock that could only be opened with a key. Her mother knew where the key was hidden but was too afraid for her own safety and for Nuala's to let her daughter out of the house. Dan had an excellent intelligence network, and he would find out if Nuala was out of the house without permission. Not only was this prison regime ensuring that Nuala did not escape – it also served to break her spirit and to erode her resistance to the match. In his softer moments, Dan would tell her that this was a marvellous chance for her to get her hands on a lot of wealth. It was a chance in a million that could not be passed up. She would have a good life on a big farm and just think of the wealth she'd inherit when Paddy died.

Dan brought his daughter out of the house one evening, put her in the car and told her he was taking her to the parish priest. She was to tell the priest that she was getting married and to arrange a date. She was also to go to Confession in preparation for the sacrament of Matrimony. He carefully coached her on what to say about her relationship with Paddy. 'Tell the priest you love him,' said Dan, with the shifty look in his eye he always had when he was going to 'pull a stroke' or 'con' somebody. 'Say that you really want to marry him. Say he's the only man for you. Now, do you understand what you are supposed to say?'

'Yes, Daddy, I'll do what you say.' Nuala couldn't help feeling that the priest would need to be an awful eejit to believe a spiel like that. He hadn't exactly come down with the last shower of rain. Dan drove to the priest's house, parked in the driveway of the fine, rambling old Victorian house set in well-tended gardens and sent Nuala into the presbytery.

Father McKeague was a tough-talking priest of the old school. Like many old-style parish priests, he was a figure of great power and authority in his own community. He believed in the fundamentals of heaven and hell, and had no truck with trendy attempts to tone down teaching on awkward things like eternal damnation. The liberal pronouncements of the Second Vatican Council of the 1960s had failed miserably to turn him into a trendy priest. He was a fiery preacher who, at Mass on Sundays, did not hesitate to denounce any backsliding among his flock – especially as regards the sins of the flesh. He would also lambast those who could find money for the pub, but not for their dues to the parish. Nuala was in awe of this man, even frightened of him, and whenever he came into her classroom at the local national school and walked up and down the aisles between the desks, she and the others would be on tenterhooks. You could have heard a pin drop.

Now she was in the priest's house on her own, sitting nervously beside this formidable man in black. They talked in a book-lined study, sitting on high-backed Victorian chairs beside a bay window that looked out onto manicured lawns.

'What can I do for you, my child?'

'I'm getting married, Father. Daddy told me to come along and fix a date for the wedding.'

'You seem very young, my child. How old are you?'

'Sixteen, Father.'

'Sixteen is a very young age for a girl to get married. How long have you known your boyfriend?'

'A couple of weeks, Father.'

'What did you say?'

'A couple of weeks, Father.'

'Are you expecting a baby?'

'No, Father.'

'Who is your boyfriend?'

'Well, he's not really a boy, Father. He's in his mid-sixties.'

The priest paused and thought for a few moments. 'Your father is behind this, isn't he?'

'Yes, Father.' Nuala broke down and blurted out through her tears, 'Daddy is making me marry him. He's a farmer and he's real old. I don't want to marry him. Oh Father, I hate him. I would rather die than marry him.'

'What's the name of your, er, fiancé?'

'Paddy McGorril, Father. I think that's it anyway. He lives beyond in Dunkellin.'

'Oh my God!' The priest was silent for a while. Then he spoke softly, with a sigh. 'I know this man. I went to school with him. I grew up with him. I know how he treated his late wife, the Lord have mercy on her, the poor woman. He is not a suitable person for you to marry.'

If the priest felt slighted by Nuala's description of his contemporary as 'real old' he gave no sign. They sat in silence for a while. She was conscious of the ticking of the clock on the mantelpiece. Nuala was too shy to ask the priest about Paddy's late wife, and what Paddy was supposed to have done to her. A frisson of fear ran through her body. What kind of man was this? What would he do to her if he had her under his control?

The priest spoke to her, trying to reassure her. She was seeing a soft, kind side to him that she never realised was there.

'Please be assured of one thing, Nuala – there is no way that I am going to perform this wedding. It is totally out of the question. This wedding will never go ahead. No priest will marry you to this man against your will.'

'Thanks, Father.'

'Your daddy – he's outside in the car, isn't he?'

Nuala nodded.

Fr McKeague got up from his chair and, beckoning Nuala to come with him, swept out of the house and down the drive, looking very much a figure of old-fashioned clerical authority in his long, black soutane. Nuala scurried along behind him. Sheepishly, she got into her father's car, and the priest began talking to Dan. She was terrified, because she knew what the consequences were going to be for her. She hadn't obeyed her father's instructions, and there would be hell to pay.

'Fair play to you, Dan,' said the priest pleasantly.

'Good evening, Father.'

'So Nuala is about to give us the big day.'

'She is indeed, Father.'

'She's a fine girl, God bless her.'

'She certainly is, Father, thanks be to God.'

'Is this the big one, Dan? Is this the big killing?'

'What do you mean?'

'I think you know what I mean.'

'Did you make a date for the wedding, Father?'

'Dan, I didn't think that even you would do it. McGorril, of all people.'

'Are you going to marry her or are you not?'

'You must know as well as I do the kind of man he is. How could you do that to your own daughter? Especially in the light of what happened to his late wife.'

'Are you refusing to marry her? Is that it?'

'I will tell you one thing, Dan, she will never walk down that aisle.'

'She bloody well will, you know.'

'Not while I have anything to do with it.'

Like most people in rural Ireland, Dan was normally deferential to the Catholic clergy. But if a priest riled him, there were no holds barred. Dan suddenly dropped the mask of politeness and respect. The evening air became filled with the sounds of what is sometimes politely described in Ireland as 'effing and blinding'.

'Do you know what you can do with yourself now, Father? You can go fuck yourself.'

'You will never have an hour's luck for what you are trying to do.'

'I'm finished with you, you fucker. You won't get any more fucking Christmas or Easter dues from me. And I fucking well will get a priest to marry her!'

'You won't, you know. It will never happen.'

'She fucking will get married, and in her own parish too!'

'She will never walk down the aisle of my church with that fella, not while there is a breath in my body.'

Any fear that Nuala ever had of the priest evaporated. She loved him after that, and was so grateful for the way he stood up for her. She idolised him. To her, he sat next to God. She was terrified of her father but the priest didn't have the slightest glimmer of fear of him. She felt that Fr McKeague was afraid of nobody, fair play to him.

A raging Dan started the car, gunned the engine and propelled the vehicle at high speed down the driveway, almost knocking down the priest in the process. Around the corner, out of sight of the presbytery, he slammed on the brakes, turned around and drove his fist with full force into Nuala's face, telling the wailing teenager, 'When I get you home you're dead.'

She wondered if her jaw had been broken by the force of the blow. It was to be sore for days afterwards. Dan was like a simmering volcano as he drove home. She was shivering with fear at the thought of what lay in store for her. Dan hustled his daughter into the house and gave her several punches to the ribs as he pushed her into her room, telling her, 'I'll see you married to him if it's the last thing I do.' Then he locked her in. By getting Fr McKeague on her side, Nuala had won a battle, but not the war. She knew that it would be a matter of macho pride for her father not to let the priest get the better of him.

The intimidation of Nuala, which included beatings and being kept a virtual prisoner in her room, went on and on. Gradually the will to resist the match began to ebb away. Nuala had come to the conclusion that she was probably going to kill herself anyway. And if she was going to die, she reckoned that it did not matter all that much if she was going to be married off to this man who made her flesh crawl. Maybe getting married would be her chance to escape the situation in which she found herself, to escape the clutches of her father. She figured that this way, she might not be her father's property any more. Maybe it would mark the end of the intimidation, the fear, the beatings. After all, she had been assured that there would be no sex involved in this 'marriage', that she would be more of a companion than a wife. She reasoned that maybe she could tolerate being a child bride, until either she escaped, or found the means and the courage to end her life. However, the niggling thought remained – what was Paddy supposed to have done to his first wife?

One night she was roused from her sleep by her father. He ordered her to get dressed. They were going to go to another priest in another parish and this time she had better co-operate, and say what she was supposed to say. It was quite a far-off parish, neither Paddy's nor her own. Paddy would also be at the presbytery. Nuala was by now resigned to her fate. She, her father and her 'fiancé' all assembled in the parlour of the priest's house. Fr Sevron turned out to be a surprisingly young priest. He said he would see the husband-to-be first, and Paddy went off to be interviewed in the priest's study. Dan reminded his daughter one last time what she had to say when she went in to the priest to arrange the marriage and to go to Confession.

Nuala said, 'Daddy, I can't tell the priest lies.' He replied, 'Of course you can. Sure they're not really lies anyway. You can get forgiven. God will forgive you. Just tell him what I told you to say, right?'

Then it was Nuala's turn to go in to talk to the young priest.

Fr Sevron quizzed her very closely. 'Are you really sure you want to marry this man?'

'Yes, Father.' She fiddled awkwardly with her hair.

'There is a huge age gap. He is so much older than you.' The priest was looking into her eyes, trying to work out what she was really thinking. Nuala put on one of her 'inscrutable' expressions, a self-defence mechanism that she had learned to use from time to time.

'I know that, Father.'

'Have you thought it all through?'

'Yeah.' She squirmed uncomfortably.

'You have no doubts in your mind about marrying this man?'

'No.'

Nuala gave all the answers that her father had instructed her to give, and the young priest obviously felt he had no choice but to go along with the wishes of this rather unusual couple, and set a date for their wedding.

While on the surface she was going along with her father's orders, inwardly she was full of anger, resentment and apprehension. She had it in mind that she would either kill herself or kill this man she was being forced to marry. No way was she putting up with it. At one stage, while with the priest, she was tempted to say to him, 'Have you a back door?' The thought of running out of the presbytery and escaping had suddenly dawned on her. But then, where would she run to? The presbytery was in the middle of nowhere.

During the lead-up to the wedding, Nuala was driven by her father into a nearby big town. They went into a solicitor's office for a meeting. Apart from her father and the solicitor, her 'fiancé', Paddy, was there too. Some kind of legal document was signed, a kind of pre-nuptial agreement setting out the conditions attached to the forthcoming marriage. Under certain conditions, she would get the farm and the house when Paddy died. She was too young to care about this idea of inheriting or 'falling in for' the land. Pop music, discos, boyfriends, socialising with the other girls at school, passing her exams, getting a job – these were the things that were foremost in her mind, not farming, or her entitlements as a widow. During the meeting with the solicitor, both Paddy and her father reiterated that this would simply be a marriage of convenience, with no sex involved. She believes that there may even have been a clause in the agreement stating that there would be 'no physical contact'. Paddy announced piously, 'I don't want her for anything physical – just companionship.' It never occurred to her to ask what guarantee she had that he would not go back on his word.

Arrangements were made to buy a wedding dress in a local town. Nuala refused to have anything to do with this, and would not go for a fitting. The woman neighbour who had cut her hair was brought in to take her measurements. Armed with this data, Dan brought Nuala off in a car with her mother and Paddy to the shop. But Nuala refused to go in. Dan stayed in the car with his recalcitrant daughter, keeping an eye on her, while her mother and Paddy entered the store. A wedding dress was chosen and also a going-away suit. Paddy paid for everything, and the outfits were delivered later. When Nuala heard about the going-away suit, she said cheekily to her mother, 'Where am I going?' Her mother supposed that she might be going away on a honeymoon. 'Honeymoon, my foot,' fumed Nuala. 'I'm not "going away" anywhere with that thing.' She still could not believe a wedding was going to take place, let alone a honeymoon.

When word spread that a marriage had been arranged between herself and Paddy McGorril, her father began getting other inquiries from elderly men who were either bachelors or widowers and who knew of his reputation as a matchmaker. Did Dan have any more like Nuala? Did she have any sisters or cousins that might be available? Fortunately, Nuala's only sister Fidelma was too young to be given in marriage to some aged stranger. One very elderly man called around to the house and was really keen to clinch a deal to marry Nuala, but Dan had to tell him she was already spoken for, and that he didn't have anything else available just then. Nuala thought the caller was a very nice man, although he seemed terribly frail and weak. It turned out that this man, a farmer, was extremely wealthy, with lots of land, and no close relatives. Just ten days after he had tried to work out a deal for Nuala, word came through that he was dead.

When Dan heard the news he almost wept, not out of sorrow for the man's demise but out of sheer frustration. He was furious at himself for missing this golden opportunity, and cursed his bad luck. Why the hell had he not taken the offer? It would have been a nice, quick transaction with a marvellous profit, a quick killing, with no bother, no hassle. He almost went berserk in the kitchen. 'What a fuck-up,' he groaned. 'I could have been a millionaire. We could all have been rolling in it.'

Dan went down on his knees with his fists raised to the heavens and made his own personal rant to the Deity. 'Are you up there at all, God? Are you? Is there a God in heaven that would do this to me, make me lose out on a great chance like this? What did I do to deserve this? Are you listening to me at all, God, are you?'

Dan's frustration grew to breaking point when it emerged that the old man had left everything in his will to the Catholic Church. No doubt Dan thought longingly of all the good uses he could have found for the money, the gambling, the boozing and the carousing he could have done with it, instead of it going to priests and nuns who had probably never bought a pint or seen the inside of a bookie's shop in their lives.

In a way, Nuala was also frustrated at the missed opportunity. She wasn't interested in elderly farmers as boyfriends or prospective husbands, but she reckoned that if she had to be married off, why could it not have been to a nice old man with one foot in the grave who was only going to live ten days? She could have got to being a widow in less than a fortnight.

Another bachelor, a well-to-do businessman, now dead, also heard on the grapevine about the match and he approached Dan to see if Nuala might be available for him. But Dan decided to stick with Paddy. Anyway, the deal had already been signed.

Nuala was now largely cut off from her friends. When she wasn't working for Dan, she was mostly kept indoors. Dan didn't want her mixing too much with young people her own age in the run-up to the wedding. Maybe he feared that they might incite her to resist the match. But Nuala still managed to have a few words from time to time with Carmel. After Sunday Mass, before Dan could drive the family home, Nuala would grab a few moments' conversation with Carmel at the back of the church. The two of them lingered by the holy water font, taking ages to dip their fingers into the water and to bless themselves, as their neighbours filtered out of the church.

'Nuala, how come we don't see you out and about any more?' Carmel asked one Sunday. 'There was a whole big crowd down at the creamery gates the other night. There was great *craic* and we had a great laugh. I thought I'd see you there.'

'Daddy is keeping me in the house.'

'Has he gone round the twist or what?'

'You know this marriage idea I told you about? Well, he seems serious about that.'

'Ah he can't be! It must be a wind-up.'

'He even made me see a priest to arrange the wedding. Carmel, I'm getting anxious.'

'Ah don't worry, Nuala. There's no way he would go ahead with something like that. Sure how could he?'

But Nuala could sense that Carmel herself was now more worried about the match than she pretended.

As the date of the wedding loomed, Dan decided he wanted to put on a big show. Nuala was outraged when she discovered he had sent out dozens of wedding invitations to friends, relatives, neighbours and pub owners whose prosperity he had subsidised by his custom. For Nuala, this was the last straw. It was bad enough being married off to Paddy. But she was not going to be publicly humiliated in front of scores of people, including individuals like publicans whom she termed 'big shots'. In a rare show of defiance, she stood up to her father. She said, 'Daddy, if you don't cancel those invitations, I am not going to marry him. I am not going to have all these people there eyeballing me with this oul' lad. I will back out on the altar and there will be nothing you can do about it.'

Dan was not used to his orders being questioned in his own household. But to her great surprise and relief, he relented. Maybe he feared his daughter would use the ultimate weapon and refuse to say 'I do' in front of the priest in the church. That would be like dropping the atomic bomb. The scandal would really destroy him in front of his cronies – and this sixteen-year-old had her finger on the trigger. Who could say what the ungrateful little bitch might do at the last minute? He just couldn't take that chance. He was forced to contact his pals and cancel the invitations. It meant missing out on presents. He had told his daughter she would get toasters and things like that. She couldn't care less about toasters. It would be a white wedding, but a very quiet, low-key one.

One Sunday, Dan brought Nuala over to Paddy's farm. They looked at the house and walked the land with Paddy. He was eager to show off his fine residence, with its gloomy, old-fashioned furniture, the big dark kitchen with the fuel-burning range and the home-made presses and, all around the house, the broad acres of pasture. There were fields where vegetables were grown, and there was an orchard. They expected her to be impressed at the place she was moving into, but she was not interested. She didn't care how big the house was, or how many barns and outbuildings there were or how big the farm was, or how many cows and bullocks he had.

'Look at that house, look at all them acres,' said Dan to his daughter as they walked along the avenue to the house, having inspected the further reaches of the farm.

'Yeah,' said Nuala.

'That's the best of land,' said Dan. 'You're not talking bogland there.'

'Really?' she said, murmuring under her breath, 'Big deal.'

Some time before the wedding was scheduled to take place, a young man called Eric called around to Nuala's house.

Dan met him at the door.

'How are you?' said Eric pleasantly.

'Not a bother,' said Dan.

'Could I speak to Nuala?' the caller said.

'She's not here. Who wants her?'

'I'm Eric, a son of the man she's getting married to.'

'I see,' said Dan, casting a wary eye over the caller. 'Is there a problem?' He remained firmly framed in the doorway, making no move to invite Eric into the house.

'There is something important I want to tell her.'

'You can tell me. I'm her daddy.'

'I wanted to warn her about my father.'

'What's the problem with him?' said Dan, pulling on a cigarette.

'My father is a violent man. He beat my mother. And if he marries your daughter, he'll beat her too. She'll be in for a terrible time. He'll give her an awful life.'

'Right, I'll tell her that. Thanks.'

Eric was probably unaware that in his encounter with Dan he was dealing with yet another wife-beater. Obviously, the warning about Paddy cut little ice with Dan. Wasn't it the privilege, even the duty, of any real man to keep his woman in check? Dan never told his daughter about Eric's visit. She did not learn about it until a long time later.

As Eric made his departure, he gave a solemn, final warning to Dan, 'You are sending your daughter into hell.'

Dan replied, 'Would you ever go and fuck off.'

CHAPTER FIVE

THE ESCAPE ATTEMPT

'She doesn't have to go ahead with this.'

Nuala sat in the kitchen and the sentence reverberated through her mind. She could hardly believe she was hearing these words. She felt a marvellous rush of relief and euphoria. It was as if the despair of the condemned cell had given way to the rapture of a reprieve – or at least the possibility of a reprieve.

Nuala kept savouring the words in her mind, 'She doesn't have to go ahead with this.'

The woman who spoke the words was Nuala's Aunt Margaret who was home on holidays from America. A kindly, generous woman, she had heard on the grapevine about the 'match' and was horrified. She knocked on the door one day, and came into the kitchen to talk to Nuala and Josey. Dan was out the back somewhere. There were just a few days to go to the wedding.

Margaret looked anxiously at Nuala sitting in the kitchen and said to Josey, 'I heard what's happening. Something has to be done.'

Margaret said that she and another of her sisters, who was home on holiday from England, would take Nuala away. Both aunts were sisters of Nuala's father. They were staying with relatives some miles away from Nuala's home. Margaret spoke to Nuala and her mother in the kitchen with great urgency. Dan could walk in at any moment and there was no time to lose.

Margaret said to Josey, 'Nuala does not have to go through with this marriage. I will take her away and rear her. I will give her the education she deserves. You will be able to see her. But the important thing now is to get her away from here. It has to be done as soon as possible.'

Nuala was on tenterhooks as she awaited her mother's response. Josey was in a dilemma. No matter what her decision was, there were dire consequences in store.

'He'll kill me,' said Josey, shaking her head. 'He'll kill her too if he catches her.'

'Oh please, Mammy, please,' said Nuala.

'You have to do it, Josey,' said Margaret quietly.

The argument went on and on, until finally Josey began to give in to the aunt's relentless pressure. In the end she breathed a deep sigh and said, 'Okay, I'll do it.'

'Oh thank Christ,' said Margaret.

'Oh Mammy,' said Nuala. 'I will never, ever forget this.'

Nuala was euphoric. It was the happiest day of her life. A plan was worked out. The following day, her aunts would be leaving the area to return home, one to America and the other to England. Josey was to bring Nuala to a certain crossroads just a few minutes' walk from their house, at a certain time. The aunts would be waiting there in a car and they were going to drive her away. Nuala did not know the exact details of the plan they had in mind. She didn't have a passport so there would have been problems about getting to America straight away. Possibly she would have been taken to England and then to America. She immediately began counting the hours to freedom.

She could hardly believe her good fortune. Maybe God had not forgotten her after all. At last she had a way of escape. She was going to be rescued and taken away from this nightmare. Almost at the final hour, a totally unexpected escape hatch had opened up, and she was going to make the break. She would have a new life abroad, where her father would never find her. She would never have to see him or Paddy ever again. She would have her liberty; she would be given an education, a career, a chance to travel, a great new life. It all happened so quickly her mind was in a spin. It was like a dream.

Nuala could think of nothing else but the prospect of her great escape the following day. Nuala had her tea in the kitchen that evening with her parents. She could see that her mother was tense. She was afraid her father might notice and start quizzing Josey as to what was wrong. Dan was great at finding out things. Maybe he knew already about the escape plan.

In bed that night, Nuala could not sleep. As the hours and minutes ticked by, she began to wonder if the escape would really happen. There were so many things that could go wrong. Her father might turn up at the wrong moment. Her mother might lose courage at the thought of the awful consequences for herself of letting Nuala escape, and of the consequences for Nuala if she was caught while trying to abscond. Who knows what Dan would do? There was also a powerful emotion gnawing away at her – a sense of guilt. How could she run away and leave her mother alone to face the awful revenge that Dan would take?

The word from the aunts was that Nuala would not have to bring anything with her when she was making her getaway. She would simply have to make the break in the clothes in which she was standing, and they would look after everything. The getaway time was fixed for a certain hour in the afternoon. Dan was around the house in the morning, but he would be absent in the afternoon, although not necessarily far away. When Nuala woke up that morning she had a mixture of feelings. On the one hand, she was euphoric at the prospect of escape, and was psyching herself up to get out of the house, get to the aunts' car and disappear. But at the same time she was on tenterhooks at the thought that something might go wrong and she still felt guilty.

After breakfast, Dan made sure that Nuala was locked into her room. Some time after her father left the house, her mother went against Dan's instructions and unlocked the door of the bedroom and let her out. But the front door was still locked. Her mother knew where the key was hidden. It was the only way out of the house. There was no back door.

Nuala's intuition began playing havoc with her peace of mind. Somehow, she sensed that her mother was getting afraid, not just for herself but for her daughter. Nuala could understand that. There were so many things that could go wrong. Her father might come along at the wrong moment and catch them in the act of absconding. If Dan was sufficiently outraged and had enough booze on board, there was no telling what he would do. He could cause serious physical injury not only to his wife but to his daughter too. Nuala knew that these considerations must have been preying on her mother's mind. And even if the escape was successful, how could her mother explain it away to Dan when he came home? He had invested so much time and trouble in this marriage it was almost as if he was tying the knot himself. Her mother would really be in for it.

Despite all the dangers, the alternative for Nuala just did not bear thinking about. If she did not make her getaway today, she would be married off the following weekend. As the minutes ticked away, Nuala kept trying to get reassurance from her mother. 'Mammy, you are letting me go, aren't you?' Her mother would nod and say 'Yes', but somehow she did not seem convincing. Josey had become very quiet and very subdued, and Nuala began to fear the worst.

As the deadline for departure approached, panic began to well up inside the teenager. Nuala kept crying and saying, 'Mammy, will you leave me out? Can I go? Mammy, when I'm on my feet and when I get older I will look after you. You will never be short. Mammy, please open the door. Please!' With a sense of doom and foreboding, Nuala began to realise that her mother was losing courage. Then, as the minutes ticked away to the deadline, the distraught mother broke the news – she could not help Nuala to escape.

'Your father is up the main street somewhere. I just know it. What will he do if he catches us? What will he do to you? Nuala, I just can't do it. Somebody could be killed. I would prefer to see you alive and married than dead in a ditch.'

Nuala cried and cried and begged her mother to open the door, but Josey was too upset and terrified to do anything. She sat motionless in a chair in the kitchen with a fixed stare, almost as if she was frozen to the spot. As the deadline for her escape came and went, Nuala sat in a corner of the kitchen and wept, her shoulders heaving up and down with the sobs.

She could imagine the car at the crossroads, her aunts waiting there, maybe with the engine running, anxiously scanning the road for any sign of her, maybe waiting long beyond the deadline in case she had been delayed and then, when they could delay no longer, driving off, confused and dejected, to make their own travel connections. As there was no phone in Nuala's house, the aunts had no way of making contact for a last-minute check that the escape was going according to plan. Nuala was never to see her Aunt Margaret again. The woman who tried to rescue her is now dead. For Nuala, losing the chance to make her getaway was one of her darkest hours.

A long time later, Dan somehow found out about his sisters' plan to 'spring' Nuala, and it led to a bitter rift. The two women came home for a family funeral, and there was only a hostile silence between them and Dan. They did not want to have anything to do with him nor he with them. Nuala was married at this stage, and she did not meet her aunts during their visit home. There seemed to be nothing further they could do to help her.

Nuala was a very good runner, and if she had got out of the house at all that day she would have taken off and escaped. She knew a short cut across the fields to the crossroads where her aunts were waiting, and she might have taken that route. At one stage she thought even of putting her head through the glass of the window in her room. All the windows in the house were old and stuck to their frames by layers of paint and could not be opened properly. And, of course, her own window had been nailed down as an additional precaution.

If Nuala had managed to make the break that day, the whole course of her life would have been different. But somehow a sense of guilt about leaving her mother to an uncertain fate had undermined her will to smash her way out of the house.

Shortly after this failed escape attempt, Nuala's summer holidays came to an end, and she returned briefly to her convent secondary school. Classes were not being held, but pupils were being prepared for the following term, and were being told what classes they would be in and what books they would need. Nuala was in a daze of depression after failing to make a break to freedom. Her father drove her to and from school. He warned her to tell nobody she was shortly going to be a married woman.

Nuala didn't like school usually, but it was better than being at home. She was relieved to get out of the oppressive home environment even for a few hours. She would only have a couple of days in school. On the Saturday, she was due to get married. She hoped to continue her education after marriage – if she didn't commit suicide in the meantime, and it was looking increasingly likely that she *would* take her own life.

She didn't tell the nuns about her wedding. Somehow, she couldn't fully believe that this marriage to an old guy was really going to happen. Anyway, she didn't really feel like confiding in the nuns. She felt she didn't have a great rapport with them, and usually sat at the back of the class, keeping a low profile.

She was delighted to see her pal Carmel again. In a corridor in the school, before going into the classroom, they had a hurried, whispered conversation.

'It's just a couple of days now,' said Nuala. 'Everything is arranged – the church, the hotel, the whole bloody lot. Oh Carmel, I'm really scared.'

'Oh my God,' gasped Carmel, horror in her eyes. 'But there is still time. Maybe he won't go through with it.'

Carmel had by now abandoned any pretence that Dan might be joking. She knew that Dan was in deadly earnest about the match, and that they were in the final countdown to the wedding day. She was just going through the motions of holding out some slight ray of hope to her pal. Nuala told her friend how her escape attempt had ended in failure. When she heard that, Carmel gave up. Always so upbeat and optimistic, Carmel, for once, failed to come up with reasons to be cheerful.

The next day, Nuala's last day at school, there was another hurried conference in the corridor between Nuala, Carmel and a couple of other girls that they were friendly with, Pauline and Grace. Nuala told them that her father was still going ahead with the match, and the other girls listened open-mouthed with horror and fascination.

'I'd commit suicide. That's what I'd do,' said Grace.

Carmel looked at her scathingly. 'Thanks a whole bloody lot, Grace. That's really helpful. Now would you suggest she do it by poison or hanging?'

'Sorry,' said Grace.

'Maybe you should tell the nuns, Nuala,' said Pauline. 'Sister Alfonsus is not the worst.'

'Oh my God, no. My father wouldn't pay any attention to them, and he'd blame me for tipping them off. I'd be in for a hiding and I'd still be married off.'

'Run away, Nuala,' said Carmel. 'That's what I'd do. Maybe your father won't go through with it. Maybe he'll pull out at the last minute. But you can't take that chance. Just run for it. Now. Before he arrives to collect you. Just get to hell out of here. You have very little time left. It's four o'clock, for Jaysus sake. He'll be here in ten minutes.'

'But where can I go? Where can I hide? I have no money. If I run away and the guards find me, I'll be brought home again.'

For once, Carmel had come up with a totally impractical solution. Maybe it was due to panic. The minutes were ticking away. Shortly, Dan would be waiting outside the school in his car, his eagle eye on the lookout for Nuala.

Pauline looked out through the window. 'I can see the car coming,' she said.

Carmel embraced Nuala and the two of them cried. The other girls also broke down. They stayed with Nuala until the last minute, until it was time for her to go. 'I'll be there tomorrow, Nuala,' said Carmel. The girls felt frightened as they watched Nuala walk out of the school and get into her father's car. It was a Friday. It was to be Nuala's last day in school. As she got into the car for the journey home, it would be her last time ever to wear a school uniform. The following day she would be in a wedding dress. The car moved off and the girls watched it until it disappeared from sight.

The day of the wedding ceremony is etched forever into Nuala's memory. Ignatius, one of her brothers who was living in England, came home and was best man. His wife, whom Nuala is still very fond of, was bridesmaid. There was nothing her brother and his wife could have done to stop the proceedings. Nuala has never blamed them for being roped in. Nuala's sister-in-law helped her with the wedding dress. Even then, putting on the dress, Nuala thought her father might not go through with it.

Conor was not around for Nuala's big day. He had emigrated a couple of weeks before the wedding. His departure meant that the guests consisted merely of Ignatius and his wife, Dan and Josey, and Nuala's sister Fidelma. Nuala never realised her former chaperone was leaving home. She came into the kitchen for the usual breakfast of porridge, tea and bread and butter one morning and noticed he wasn't there. She hadn't seen him at tea the previous evening either. When she asked, 'Where's Conor?' Dan simply said, 'Oh, Conor, he went to England yesterday.' Conor was always a lad of few words.

Nuala got so drunk at the wedding reception that she has no recollection of how she got back home to her parents' house. She reckoned she must have been carried bodily into the house from a car and thrown onto her bed. The next morning she woke up in her own room, lying on her bed, fully clothed in her wedding dress, and with a ferocious hangover. As she awoke with the sun streaming in through the window, she hoped against hope that she had simply been having a nightmare, and that this hideous wedding would prove to be just a figment of her imagination. Then the awful realisation grew that she had not been dreaming, and that she was well and truly trapped. In the eyes of church and state, except in certain exceptional cases, marriage was forever. It was as if a life sentence had just been imposed upon her. In retrospect, she would almost certainly have received a church annulment had she sought one. Annulments were becoming more common in the Ireland of the 1970s. But she knew nothing of such matters.

Her mother came into the bedroom and gently reminded her that she was now a married woman, and would no longer have to stay at home. She would go to her husband's house. Nuala shuddered when she realised that Paddy was already there, waiting to claim his 'prize', waiting to take her away in his car. It was as if the barbarians were already inside the gates. She moaned to herself, 'Oh my God.'

Her father was tough-minded as usual. He told her sternly, 'You're going to have to go with him now, right?'

She was quite a sight as she came into the kitchen to join her parents and meet her new lord and master. She was dishevelled, ferociously hung over and still in the rumpled wedding dress that she had slept in. It wasn't exactly the image that Dan had hoped to project of Nuala as a paragon of discipline and domestic virtue. Her father was fuming and hissed at her, 'The state of you!' Both he and the husband were giving out to her over getting drunk. She had no breakfast. She did not feel like eating. She had never felt so sick. Between the hangover and the thought of being married to this man, all she wanted was to lie down and die. While Paddy was given something to eat, she went away, cleaned up, brushed her hair, and, as instructed, put on her new 'going away' suit. Her mother wept as she packed her daughter's toiletries and other possessions, including the wedding dress, into a case for this journey into an uncertain new life. What other few clothes she possessed had already been transferred to Paddy's house.

She felt as if she was being taken away to a condemned cell as she was driven off with Paddy in his car, sitting glumly in the front seat, staring directly ahead. She squirmed with disgust as he put his hand on her leg, telling her, 'You'll be happy now, Nuala.'

She thought silently to herself, 'What do you know or care about my happiness, you bastard!'

The first thing he did that morning was take her to Mass in his parish church. Like most farmers of his generation and in that region, he was conventionally religious, never missing Sunday Mass. But Nuala believed he had another purpose in mind that morning – to show off his new trophy, his teenage bride. He accompanied her up along the centre aisle to the very top of the church, in full view of the congregation, just before the Mass began. He was a well-known figure in the small parish, and everybody in the little stone church stood up and applauded the local man and his new wife. She almost expected somebody to call out, 'Fair play to you, Paddy, for snagging a young one.'

Nuala felt as if he was saying to them all, 'Look what I got.' Everybody was staring at her. She was the centre of attention, almost as if she was the Princess of Wales. She was deeply embarrassed and resentful. She was astonished when the people stood up and applauded. She never saw that happening before or since. She wished the ground would open up and swallow her. During the Mass, the priest congratulated the couple and wished them years of happiness. She thought to herself, 'Some happiness!'

Paddy drove his young wife back to the house after Mass. As she got out of the car, Lassie ran to her and jumped around her, yelping a welcome. She was pleased that Lassie remembered her – but even Lassie and the warmth of his welcome failed to lift her spirits. Paddy showed Nuala into the kitchen and called in Sylvester, the workman. Sylvester had not known that his boss was getting married again. Sylvester looked stunned when Paddy introduced Nuala to him saying, 'This is my wife.' Nuala would never forget the expression on Sylvester's face. He often told her afterwards how he was taken totally by surprise. The husband gave him a drink that day to celebrate. She was not given one. In any case, she was so sick from the hangover she thought she would never drink again. The husband showed her around the house. She was shown her room and got settled in. She noticed there was a lock on the door of her bedroom, but no sign of any key. She wished she had a way of securing the door against intruders, just to be on the safe side.

The very next day, a Monday, Nuala's father Dan acquired a brand new car, a Morris Mini, at a local garage. She saw him driving it and was mystified as to how he had managed to buy it. The car was worth about £850. She knew that, despite his wheeler-dealer abilities and his qualities as a salesman, he was broke. Too much of his spare cash went on drink and gambling. So where had he found the resources to buy a new car?

CHAPTER SIX

THE NEWLY-WEDS

At first, Paddy acted like a perfect gentleman towards his young bride. She was relieved that she had been given her own room, and she soon set to work decorating it with photos and posters of David Essex. She reasoned that if she was going to be forced to live in this house, she might as well try to make it comfortable and appealing for the time she was there. A big circular staircase led down from her room to the ground floor, and when nobody was looking she would slide down the banisters. She was still a child at heart. She didn't really feel like a married woman, and only had a vague idea about the facts of life. She had discreetly asked one of her aunts about sex, which was not a normal subject for discussion in her own home. 'Auntie, when two people get married, what happens?' The aunt gave Nuala a broad, and not terribly detailed outline of what sexual intercourse meant. Nuala was aghast. 'Surely I won't have to do that? Daddy says I won't have to do that.' The thought of making love to this old man whom she had been forced to marry terrified and disgusted her. Again she tried to reassure herself that she had been promised there would be no physical contact in this marriage. She was encouraged that this promise would be kept when Paddy showed her to her room at the top of the house where she would be sleeping – alone. His room was just across the landing.

She was wary at first about Sylvester, the second man in the house. A kitchen had been built on to the side of the house, and Sylvester lived in a small attic over the kitchen, with one tiny window. He would enter his dingy eyrie by means of a door in the upper gable wall, and to reach the door he had to climb up a ladder from the farmyard. There was no electricity in his tiny room, which was lit only by an oil lamp in the hours of darkness. He had no heating either, except what percolated up from the range in the kitchen. When Nuala moved in at first, she wasn't sure what to make of him. Just to be on the safe side, she decided to get her retaliation in first. 'If you touch me, I'll kill you,' she told the startled Sylvester when she got him alone. In fact, he turned out to be a perfect gentleman, and a bond of friendship developed between them. Each was a kind of exile living in an alien world that hadn't done either of them many favours.

Sylvester appeared to have few close living relatives. He had been living for many years in the county home and was now slaving on the farm for a mere pittance of £3 a week.

Before Nuala arrived in the house, Sylvester had to buy his own food out of his miserable weekly allowance. He would buy bread and luncheon roll or corned beef in the local shop, and make up a sandwich and eat it at the table in the kitchen, or he might buy a few rashers and cook them. Nuala tried to give him the semblance of a decent life, making sure he got decent, hot food, and letting him into the house to watch the TV and sit in front of the fire when Paddy's back was turned. Normally Sylvester was confined to the kitchen and the attic. The teenage wife and the workman performed small kindnesses for each other, giving each other sweets and cigarettes whenever one had something and the other was short. Nuala had an outgoing personality and a barbed, irreverent wit, and Sylvester was delighted and amused by her. She brought laughter into the workman's dreary life, and they enjoyed many a joke together.

Sylvester came to enjoy being with this lively teenage girl who was like a creature from a different planet. Nuala would rather freeze in the kitchen at night talking to Sylvester than sit in the parlour in front of the fire and the TV with the husband. When the coast was clear, she would bring Sylvester in for a chat at night in the big gloomy house where you could hear the echoes if you shouted. Or if the husband was there she would sometimes ask permission to bring Sylvester in. Sylvester could not read, and if there was something in the newspaper that he was interested in, Nuala would read it for him. She got him a radio from her own family home and she put lino down on the floor of his room – it was a dark, depressing room, and she could not bear to be there. She felt they had things in common. She had no life and he had no life – he was put into this world for slavery, she reckoned. She used to say to him, 'Why don't you just leave here? Why don't you try to go away and make a life for yourself?' And he would say, 'But where can I go? Sure I have nowhere to go.' Paddy would keep him in line by threatening him, 'You're going back into the home!'

Nuala's other friend on the farm was Lassie. She lavished her love on the sheepdog. She felt that Lassie, in turn, loved her. She always loved the way that Lassie came dashing up to her to welcome her home whenever she came up the avenue. She felt that Lassie had never really been shown affection before, and that the animal was responding to her own display of devotion to him. She gave more affection to Lassie than to the husband.

Nuala had been taught to cook from an early age, and the arrangement was that she would do some cooking and light household duties in her new home. There were two other women who came in to work in the house from time to time. One acted as a kind of housekeeper and the other as a cleaner. Nuala did not get on well with the house-keeper, and they disagreed about the running of the kitchen. The housekeeper was a lady of mature years, and it was perhaps under-standable that she would take exception to suggestions from a mere schoolgirl who had suddenly invaded her domain. Nuala was furious at the housekeeper's attitude towards her, and then one night in bed she had a brainwave – she would pull rank. The next morning the sixteen-year-old assumed what she hoped was an air of authority and told the astonished housekeeper, 'There's something I have to ex-plain to you, missus. I'm the boss's wife. I'm the woman of the house. You do not tell me what to do. I tell you what to do. Do I make myself clear?' The poor housekeeper was speechless. It was probably the first time Nuala had ever given orders to an adult, and she got a great kick out of it. She reckoned she might as well get some benefit from being married, albeit forcibly, to the master of the house. The house-keeper and the cleaner stopped coming around after a few days.

By comparison with her family home in the middle of a village, where there was the constant noise of people talking and passing by, Nuala found her new home eerily quiet and isolated. It was only about fifteen minutes' walk to the nearest village of Dunkellin, but the house was quite remote from any other habitation. Dunkellin itself was like many another village in the region – a narrow main street, terraced rows of two-storey, slate-roofed houses that opened onto the footpath, a selection of pubs and shops, a Catholic church with a graveyard and a post office.

Despite the proximity of the village, Paddy's home seemed to Nuala to be one of the most lonely, out-of-the-way places she had ever encountered. She realised that some people would like the soli-tude and the quietness, but she found it spooky. She would hear a dog bark occasionally, or a cow lowing, or the crows, or the wind in the trees, or the distant sound of a car, and that was all. When she first went there, she would leave the light on in her room at night. It was out of fear of the husband. She had this terrible dread that he would come into her room. He was still a virtual stranger to her even though she was married to him.

In a way, the husband treated her like a child. He would take her by the hand and show her around the fine big house and the farm, and show her the animals. It was mainly a dairy farm. He tried to teach her how to milk a cow but that was one thing she just could not handle. She took one look at the animal and ran away. She was frightened of cows, even though she had grown up in the country. Also, she had no interest in cows or farming. She was more interested in pop music and going to dances.

She could imagine being chatted up by a young fella at a dance.

'What do you do?' he would say.

'I milk cows.'

She loved feeding calves but reckoned that it was not really farming – more a question of looking after pets. She really loved the calves. She thought they were so endearing, so innocent.

Paddy also owned land a couple of miles away from the house, and there was a hill at the top of those fields. One day he brought her up to the top of the hill, pointed to his land and said, 'All this will be yours one day, Nuala.'

The teenager looked at her fingernails and said, 'Yeah.'

Maybe her husband had attitudes from a previous generation and had assumed that any woman from a less well-off background should feel privileged to marry into a big house and a big farm that, in the natural course of events, she would inherit after his death. She was moving from penury into prosperity. Instead of living in a rundown cottage she was residing in an elegant country house as the wife of a well-to-do farmer. Surely she ought to be grateful for that? What more could she want? The problem for Paddy was, Nuala was very much a girl of the modern age, who believed in the concept of romantic love and in the freedom to choose who she wanted to fall in love with. She had the temerity to believe that she should have had the liberty to select the man who would become her husband, rather than have others make the choice for her. She felt that Paddy had used his wealth to bypass the normal conventions of modern courtship. Instead of trying to win the heart of a woman fair and square, he had dealt instead with her father who was abusing his parental authority by forcing her into marriage. She felt that Paddy, in effect, had cheated.

She was resentful that nobody ever asked her what she wanted. Her father had never asked her if she wanted to marry Paddy. And Paddy had never asked her if she wanted to marry him. Nuala felt she was like something Paddy had seen in a shop window that he wanted to have and decided to put a deposit on. There was no such thing as a proposal of marriage. In fact she made it clear to her father that she did not want to marry this man, but was totally ignored. Even though it was her entire life that was at stake, her wishes were not taken into account in the slightest. She had had as much say in this match as a heifer being bought and sold at a mart.

After moving into the husband's house, Nuala was kept under close supervision, like a child. If she used a four-letter word, or smoked, the husband would phone her father or call to see him and tell him. Dan would come down to the house almost every second night to watch her and make sure she was behaving herself. Dan had a lot of influence over the husband. For instance, Dan did not want

Nuala to see the teenage friends she had before she married, and he told the husband to make sure she did not mix with them. Whatever her father said, went. The husband would say to Nuala, 'Your father said you were to do this or that.' Even though Nuala was married, she was still under her father's control.

When her father would visit Paddy's house in the evening, Josey would often come too, and Nuala would sit talking to her in the kitchen while Dan and the husband were drinking in the sitting room. Josey would be hoping Nuala would not provoke her father, warning her, 'You know what he is like.' She would try to console Nuala by saying, 'This is not going to last forever.' Dan continued to be Nuala's master and of course she had now picked up a second master – the husband. She got away with the occasional display of disobedience but mostly she had to do whatever they told her to do. Neither of them would have known anything about Women's Lib or feminism. Nuala was vaguely aware of feminism at the time – there was mention on TV about women burning their bras in America. But she did not feel it was relevant to her.

One day an old-fashioned, black Hillman Hunter car came slowly up the avenue and parked in front of the house. There were two nuns inside. One of them got out and came up the steps to the front door. It was Sr Alfonsus, Nuala's former teacher. Nuala showed her into the sitting room. Nuala's mother was visiting at the time and she went to the kitchen to get tea and biscuits. Paddy and Sylvester were away from the house. The nun got straight to the point, when she and Nuala were alone.

'Nuala, I never knew you were getting married. Why didn't you tell us?'

'It's a long story, sister.'

'There are all kinds of rumours going around.'

'If you're asking me was I forced into it, the answer is yes.'

'You should have come to us.'

'Well, it's too late now.'

'You were doing well at school. You could always come back.'

'They don't want me to go back.'

'You could have passed all the exams. You wanted to be a nurse, didn't you?'

'I wanted to nurse old people. Instead of that I married one.'

Perhaps with the reminder of what might have been, Nuala began to sob. 'I'm sorry,' she said, wiping her eyes.

'That's all right,' said the nun. 'Take your time.'

'How did you find me, sister?'

'There are few secrets in Knockslattery.'

The nun was sympathetic, but Nuala could tell that, like so many others in the Ireland of that era, clerical and lay, her former teacher considered that marriage was for life, that it was for better or for worse. The nun tried to be tactful but Nuala could see she did not give the marriage much of a chance. 'It might work out,' said the nun. Her parting comment was not very encouraging either – 'I'll get a Mass said for you.'

Nuala learned that the nun also called around to confront her father. She heard all about it from her mother. With long practice in giving tongue-lashings to errant schoolgirls, the angry sister laid into Dan with gusto for forcing Nuala into this marriage. 'You're an absolute brute for doing this to your daughter,' Sr Alfonsus told him. Dan couldn't care less what she said. The marriage was an accomplished fact, the deal had been done, and everything else was just hot air. He told her, 'Because you're wearing a habit doesn't mean you can give me orders. Now fuck off out of here.'

Nuala had wanted to continue with her education with the nuns after marriage. Her father had promised her that she could go back to school as a married woman. But after the wedding it was a different story. Neither her father nor her husband wanted her to resume her studies. Maybe they figured a farmer's wife didn't need educational qualifications. Or, more likely, they reckoned that if Nuala went back to school, it would only emphasise the fact that Paddy had married a schoolgirl. Paddy probably didn't relish the idea of having his wife parading around in a school uniform. For whatever reason, Nuala's formal education had come to an end, although she was to continue to try to educate herself through reading. For Nuala, it was just another betrayal.

Paddy liked to make out that she was older than she really was, but Nuala firmly refused to play along with this charade. She took a malicious delight in telling the brutal truth about her age to any neighbour who cared to inquire. One of her first trips outside Paddy's house was to a shop in the nearby village of Dunkellin. A number of local farmers' wives were there, buying groceries and chatting among themselves. There was a sudden hush as Nuala walked in. The teenager was the centre of attention.

'Oh it's Nuala, Paddy's new wife. And how are you, Nuala? You're a fine young girl ... And what age are you, Nuala?'

Nuala replied truthfully, 'I'm sixteen going on seventeen.'

There was a sharp intake of breath among the women and a lot of sly glances exchanged. One of them said, 'But Paddy says you're nineteen.'

'No, that's not true. I'm sixteen going on seventeen.'

She was an avid reader of teenage girls' magazines and had her favourite ones on order in the shop. She would scour them for any photos or posters of her heart-throb, David Essex, and she would carefully cut these out and collect them. Sometimes, like a child, she would buy a lollipop in the shop and once returned to the house still sucking it. When her husband saw her with the lollipop, he went berserk. He grabbed it from her and dumped it, saying, 'You're a married woman now. Stop behaving like a child.' She sobbed, 'But I am a child, aren't I?' She kept on buying lollipops, but learned to hide them from the husband.

Despite the fact that she had been bullied into this loveless union, Nuala was certainly not the doormat type, and from time to time, even in this forced marriage, her feisty character would shine through – especially one time when Paddy bought her a pair of wellington boots. She was outraged and insulted. She saw this as the first step in the process of turning her into a farmer's wife, a role she just was not interested in playing. To her the wellies symbolised the start of the slippery slope down to life-long servitude on the farm, and she was not having it. She took immediate and direct action and threw the offending footwear into the fire, declaring to her husband, 'You're not turning me into a farmer's wife.' Oddly, Paddy saw the funny side of the incident and laughed. It was at a stage when she was still being treated with kid gloves. Nuala had seen other farmers' wives around the area and was singularly unimpressed. They seemed to her to be rather dowdy, boring creatures immersed in a life of drudgery and smelling of cow dung. This young girl with a passion for pop music and the latest fashions certainly did not want to be like them.

For their part, some of the local farmers' wives didn't think much of Nuala either. She heard on the grapevine that one of them was even accusing her own husband of taking too much of an interest in Paddy's attractive new teenage wife. 'That one have the husband gone mad!' she declared. In the local grocery shop, a few of the local women would gossip about her, sometimes within her hearing. 'Will you look at your one, she's only a tart!' Nuala would pretend not to be hurt and she would stride out of the shop with her head held high and with a broad smirk. But in reality she was stung by the barbs, and would sometimes be in tears on her way home.

Paddy would buy the *Farmer's Journal* every week, and he would pass it on to her. 'Read that,' he would say. 'You have to learn how to be a farmer's wife.' He also tried to get her to join the Irish Country-women's Association. There was no way she wanted to belong to that very worthy group. She just could not imagine herself mixing with farmers' wives.

In the early, honeymoon period of the marriage, Nuala was pampered. She got almost anything she wanted. It didn't turn the marriage into a happy one, but at least it made life bearable. When she first came to Paddy's house there was only an outside toilet, and this certainly did not meet with her approval. Paddy quickly had a bathroom installed in what used to be a pantry off the kitchen. He also had a phone put in, but he was careful with money and made sure to keep the instrument locked in a cupboard when he was away from the house. There was no TV in the house when she arrived first, and Paddy arranged to buy one. They could only get the Irish station, RTÉ, and Paddy always wanted to turn off the set at about 9.30 in the evening.

Nuala told Paddy she would love a donkey, and there was a neighbour in her own family's district with one for sale. Paddy bought the animal, but it turned out to be a jackass that didn't take kindly to being ridden. It threw Nuala on her first attempt to get up on its back. That evening, Paddy killed the jackass with a shotgun blast. Nuala was really upset, and cried for the poor animal. 'Sure it was in his nature to throw me off,' she explained to her mother.

Paddy would make sure that her favourite shampoo and deodorants would be bought for her. She liked chocolate, and Paddy would bring her boxes of Milk Tray. That was a real luxury. She was allowed on shopping trips with her mother to buy clothes. Mini-skirts were in fashion at the time. She had a good body, and had kept fit with tennis and running, and she thought she looked well in minis. She would be required to 'model' her new clothes for her husband. He would look at her admiringly and compliment her saying, 'You look lovely.'

On trips back to her family home with her mother, Nuala would slip out of the house and call to see her pal Carmel, wearing her new clothes and secretly looking forward to the compliments she knew she'd get.

'Nuala, you're looking a million dollars. Give us a twirl.'

'Your man paid for the outfit. And the make-up.'

'Jaysus, he must be loaded. Mammy is still waiting for the next sale to buy me a pair of jeans. Now the only problem is this – if he is giving you all these things, what's he looking for in return?'

'What do you mean?'

'What about the bould thing? Is he looking for that?'

'He can look all he wants – he won't get it.' They laughed. Nuala went on, 'Oh there's an agreement on that. That's all sorted. I've been given guarantees and everything. I'm just a companion, like. I have my own room and all.'

'So a ride's out of the question,' grinned Carmel.

'Bloody sure!'

'So what's it really like living out there?'

'Actually, I'm bored out of my skull. There are some lovely little calves. Real dotes, and I love feeding them. And there's a sheepdog, Lassie, that I adore and Lassie adores me and goes everywhere with me. Lassie is a "he" even though he has a girl's name. Inside the house there's a great banisters that you can slide down. I get to go jogging now and then but apart from that and a little housework, there is really nothing to do. Talk about being in the middle of nowhere!'

Nuala produced a paper bag and handed it to Carmel. 'There's a few Milk Tray for you.'

Carmel's eyes opened wide with delight. 'Oh Nuala you're a star.'

'Your man bought them too,' said Nuala.

Carmel looked at the chocolates. 'Fair play to you, Nuala, you put in the nice ones too – I hate those ones with the hard toffee centres.'

'Sure didn't I always know you hated toffee.'

As Carmel sampled the chocolates, Nuala asked shyly, 'How's Larry? Any word of him?'

'Haven't you heard? He's doing a strong line with that one Evelyn. I think she always fancied him.'

Nuala felt a secret stirring of regret.

Paddy was extremely proud of his young, attractive new wife. He liked to show her off. He would take her to pubs and to local dances, and she would be the centre of attention. Sometimes people would think she was Paddy's daughter – or granddaughter. At social events young fellas would come up to him and say, 'Can I dance with your daughter?' That used to drive him up the wall. He used to interrogate her, 'Did you tell him to say that?' He would tell her who to dance with and who not to dance with. Sometimes, for an old-time waltz, he would say to her, 'Come on and we'll dance.' She always knew then what was going to happen – the floor would clear so that they could all get a good look at her and him together. They would be saying, 'Look at your one with the oul' fella.' She felt like going through the floor with embarrassment.

After Nuala married Paddy, there was a stream of visitors to the house – mostly old farmers eager for a glimpse of Paddy's attractive new wife. Most were just inquisitive, a few mildly lecherous. Nuala was a curiosity to them. Farmers for miles around, some of them old bachelors, dropped in for a visit, including men who had not called for years. Paddy used to say, 'They never came to visit me until you came into the house.'

Paddy also brought her to a couple of cattle marts. She did not have a clue about cattle, and on her second visit to a mart stampeded a herd of cattle which she thought was going to attack her. Paddy stopped bringing her after that. She would be the centre of attention for the old farmers at the mart. They would flock around her like bees around honey. Some of these gap-toothed old guys would grin and give her a wink, and if Paddy wasn't looking she'd wink back, just for a laugh. In the pub, some of them would sidle up to her and say things like, 'Do you give it to him?' or 'Can I see you later?' or 'You're a fine young one.' She felt like an exhibit in a freak show.

Paddy tried to have conversations with her but the age gap between them was too wide. They really had nothing in common to talk about. They would sit silently over meals together in the kitchen. Even after several weeks in the house, they were like complete strangers to each other.

She tried to keep reasonably busy by looking after the kitchen and doing some household chores. She did not believe in working to excess, and her mother would help out during her frequent visits. The advantage of keeping reasonably active was that it helped to stave off the sense of boredom that hung about her constantly like a cloud. Life in the big house, away from her friends and the normal pursuits of young people, was tedious. Some of the household chores she saw as a challenge. There was a beautiful mahogany table in the dining room and she loved to polish it, and see the shine come up.

Even though Nuala was technically the boss's wife, she felt she had no real status in the household. Apart from the occasional minor grocery item that she would buy in one of the local stores, Paddy did all the shopping, usually on his way home from the creamery, and decided what they would eat. She couldn't stand the hairy bacon that he always seemed to buy. The farm was largely self-sufficient in terms of vegetables, and through his contacts with local farmers' wives, Paddy would get a ready supply of soda bread and home-made country butter. She hated the strong flavour of the butter, and longed for the smoother taste of the shop-bought, processed variety. The occasional sliced pan or a single of chips with salt and vinegar or a burger would not have gone amiss either. Sometimes she would cook dinner in the evening, and sometimes Paddy would do it. He always got his own breakfast, because she did not believe in getting up as early as he did – about 5.00 or 5.30 am.

Paddy said to Nuala once, 'Maybe, in time, you will come to love me.' She shrugged and said, 'Yeah.' She murmured to herself under her breath, 'When hell freezes over.' There were so many things that emphasised the chasm between them. Paddy was passionately interested in politics and was an avid supporter of Fianna Fáil. Nuala could not care less about politics or who governed the state. Paddy couldn't bear to listen to the pop music that Nuala wanted to hear on the radio, and would turn it off. She, for her part, had little interest in the news and current affairs programmes that he wanted to watch on TV. He would always be in for the 6.00pm RTÉ TV news bulletin, which is preceded by the Angelus. In accordance with the tradition for many rural people of his generation, he would stand and say the Angelus out loud. He would insist that Nuala say it as well. She was of a generation that was giving up these old rituals, and would just pretend to say the prayer. Paddy also had a puritanical streak. If they were watching a film on the television and a scene with a couple kissing came on, he would turn it off.

Nuala tried to blot the marriage out of her mind as best she could. There had been no professional photographer at the wedding, but her brother Ignatius took some photos and later delivered the prints to her. She promptly destroyed them. She reckoned it was bad enough looking at the husband in reality without looking at him in snaps. She met one of her old school friends one day and the girl gave her a bright, friendly greeting, innocently remarking, 'Nuala, how are you? And how is the husband?' Nuala went berserk and grabbed the unfortunate girl by the neck. 'Don't you ever, ever, for as long as you live, mention the word "husband" to me. Do you understand?' She rarely referred to Paddy by his first name or even as 'my husband'. The latter phrase indicated too close a degree of intimacy. He was usually 'the oul' fella' or 'the husband' or 'McGorril' or 'your man'. A few weeks into the marriage, she threw away her wedding ring. There was a fast-flowing stream near her parents' house, and she contemptuously flung the ring into the torrent and watched as it was swept away.

Nuala was a promising athlete and had done very well in school competitions. When she originally went to live in Paddy's house, she pleaded with her father, 'Daddy, I'm not giving up my running. I'll give up anything else, but please don't take that away from me, please don't let anybody stop me running.' In one of his softer moments, Dan told Paddy, 'Let her continue with her running – it's her pastime.' Going for runs was one of the things that helped to keep her sane after moving to live in Paddy's house.

In T-shirt, shorts and running shoes, Nuala would go jogging down the long avenue from the house. She loved the sense of exhilaration she got from the running, the feel of the wind in her hair, the 'high' that athletes got from vigorous exercise. Lassie would run along with her, yelping with delight at the adventure. By now, Nuala and Lassie had become almost inseparable. Lassie would be on the lookout for any sign that Nuala was going out for a walk or for a run, and would faithfully tag along with her.

Running, the love given to her by Lassie, and her 'shrine' to David Essex were among the things that helped to make life bearable in Paddy's house. Nuala would gaze longingly at her Essex posters and sigh with desire at the thought of this gorgeous hunk. Before going to bed, she would kiss his portrait goodnight, go down on her knees and virtually pray to him. Paddy had never heard of David Essex, but he gradually became aware of the pop star and his young wife's devotion to him.

He said to her one day, 'This fella David Essex, are you in love with him?'

'I most certainly am.'

'Would you sleep with him if you got the chance?'

'Of course I would!'

CHAPTER SEVEN

THE PRICE

Just a few months after her enforced marriage, Nuala was in her room one night, in her nightdress, about to go to bed, when the door opened and her husband walked in, stark naked. She was aghast, and literally dumbstruck. It was the first time she had seen a male adult in the nude. She got such a shock that she froze and could not talk. She looked in the long mirror of the wardrobe and saw him next to her, trying to charm her. She was afraid to turn around and actually look at him. He was murmuring 'I love you' and started feeling and caressing her. She hoped the ground would open up and swallow her. She wished she could die there and then. Seeing she was not responding, Paddy fell silent and went back to his own room across the landing. All that night, she never closed an eye, never slept a wink. She kept watching the door in case it would open again.

A few nights after this late-night visitation, Nuala was again in her room, in her nightdress, preparing to go to bed. She was putting another David Essex poster onto her wall, to join the collection already there. She was startled to hear the door being thrown open behind her and glanced around. There, framed in the doorway once again, was the naked figure of her elderly husband. This time, his attitude was a lot more aggressive.

Once again, she was stunned, dumbfounded. With mounting alarm she sensed real danger now.

'You're my wife,' he told her sternly. 'Lie down on that bed.'

'Get away from me,' she screamed, and began to cry.

'Get down on that bed or I will tell your daddy.'

'Leave me alone, please leave me alone,' she wailed.

Her panic escalated into a frenzy as she noticed that Paddy was not alone. He had brought back-up. A middle-aged man was hovering around outside the room armed with a number of lengths of rope, the type used as halters for farm animals. She had seen him before.

Paddy, a big strong man, lifted Nuala up and threw her down on the bed. His assistant came and helped Paddy to tie her to the bed. Paddy tied the knots on one side of the bed, and his acolyte did the same on the other side. It was like tying up a pig before slaughter. Nuala was spread-eagled, bound by the wrists and ankles. She could hardly speak with the shock. She wanted to scream and cry out with horror and panic but the sounds died in her throat. She wondered if she did manage to cry out, would the sound carry to the attic over the kitchen where Sylvester had his room.

She knew the man with the ropes had been pressurised by Paddy into taking part in this obscene ritual. She knew this man really did not want to get involved. He was full of nerves, and she could feel his hands shaking as he was tying her down. Paddy proceeded to claim his rights as a husband with all the finesse of the farmyard, with as much gentleness as a raging bull servicing a young heifer. Nuala, who had just turned seventeen, was struck dumb with shock. She will always remember how the assistant was ordered to stay in the room, and how he looked on from the shadows in a corner as she was raped. All the bedrooms in the house had sinks, and he was standing by the sink. She can still see his eyes burning into her as she was degraded in front of him. Nuala believes this associate of her husband's later suffered a crisis of conscience over his role in the assault.

She will never forget the words that Paddy spat at her during the rape, 'You slag. I bought you. I own you. You've been paid for.' This was one of the first firm indications she got that Paddy had actually paid her father a bribe for her hand in marriage.

Being raped by this man while being told that he had bought her from her own father was the lowest point of Nuala's entire life. Even the terrible things that had gone before – the indecent assaults by her father, the beatings, the intimidation – seemed to pale into insignificance by comparison with the realisation that she had been sold off as little more than a sex slave by the man who, above anybody else, should have been looking out for her interests, her own father. At one stage during the rape she managed to blurt out, 'You're not supposed to be doing this.' It was a reference to the pre-nuptial 'guarantee' that there would be no physical contact in this marriage.

Paddy didn't feel like arguing the point.

'I fucking well paid for you,' he hissed at her.

It began to dawn on her how her father had acquired the Morris Mini. Like any farmer involved in buying and selling livestock, Paddy had a clear idea of the cash value of every beast on his farm. He seemed to have the same attitude towards his wife. At later stages, Paddy would boast to Nuala about the exact price he had paid for her. Apart from the Morris Mini, he had paid Dan the sizeable cash sum of £2,500. Nuala is unclear as to when the cash was handed over, but she learned that her mother had the distasteful experience of seeing her husband triumphantly brandishing a large roll of bank notes he had received from Paddy. Josey told Nuala it was the biggest amount of cash she had ever seen in her life – in those days it was the equivalent of a year's wages for many people. Nuala could imagine her father with an exultant grin, showing off the tainted money. Nuala also learned that, just two days after her wedding, Dan had gone along with Paddy to the garage to select the Morris Mini, and that Paddy had paid for the car. Dan had delivered his side of the deal by virtually frogmarching his daughter up the aisle, and Paddy, being a man of his word, was keeping his side of the bargain.

The physical pain of the rape was excruciating. She had never gone through such physical suffering. She was in so much agony that she passed out, coming to while the rape was still in progress. Subsequently she met Paddy's shame-faced accomplice, and learned that at one stage they feared she might be dead. But even that fear was not enough to knock Paddy off his stride, once he had begun sexual intercourse. When he was finished, Paddy ordered his assistant to untie the weeping teenager. She made up her mind there and then that she was going to kill herself.

She blurted out that she was going to throw herself out the window – and she meant exactly what she said. It was quite a drop to the ground, and she would probably not have survived the fall. To stop her making a death leap, Paddy ordered that she be tied up again. This time, it was just her wrists that were tied – to the bedsprings. Then the two men withdrew. She was still bound as she drifted off into a troubled, tearful slumber. When she woke up the next morning the bonds had been removed, but the door and the windows of her room were locked. Later, she found the door unlocked and she realised that her parents were downstairs. She walked slowly and uncertainly down the stairs in her night clothes to the bathroom on the ground floor. She grabbed the banisters that she used to love to slide down, holding onto them to steady herself. She felt dirty and degraded and just wanted to die. She learned that day how a person feels after rape. She can still see herself walking slowly down those stairs, touching each step, feeling filthy. She did not want to live.

Her immediate priority was to have a bath. She wanted to wash away the dirt of the rape. Reflecting on it now, she realises just how much her life was scarred by that savage attack. For the rest of her life she would find it really difficult to have an intimate, loving relationship with a man. Paddy had robbed her of that precious gift. She spent ages having the bath, until her father came and hammered angrily on the door saying, 'What are you doing in there?'

She replied, 'I'm just having a wash.' She felt like killing him. When she came out of the bathroom, she found that her mother had left clothes outside for her. Obviously they wanted her to get dressed quickly and join them. She dressed in the bathroom, and went to meet her husband and her parents in the kitchen.

Paddy was pleasant and relaxed, behaving as if nothing had happened the night before. She found it bizarre, unreal – Paddy having a friendly chat about farming with Dan, whose daughter he had just raped. That day, the rapist took them all out to lunch in a hotel. Paddy and her father talked about Nuala all through the lunch as if she was not there. She wasn't included in the conversation and didn't seek to join in. She had nothing to say to these men. They discussed her as if she were a prize heifer – how well she was eating, what she liked to eat, the way she looked, the way she dressed. In asking about her likes and dislikes, Paddy addressed all his questions to her father. She wondered why it never occurred to him to ask her what her preferences were.

She looked silently at her father during that lunch, watched him smiling and being so pleasant and good-humoured, and thought,

'How I hate you, you bastard, for what you have done to me.' She could never forget the indecent assaults he had carried out against her as a child. She had never told anybody about that, and had always hated her father for what he had done to her. Now he had forced her into a situation where she had been raped. She knew in her heart that it was not going to be just a question of a single, once-off attack. It was going to happen again and again. All she wanted now was a way out. Suicide was on her mind that day. She felt that if she could have got her hands on a gun she would have blown her own brains out without hesitation.

When Nuala got her mother alone in the ladies, she blurted out the story about how she had been tied down and raped the night before. Her mother groaned, buried her face in her hands and broke down. She embraced her daughter and the two clung to each other until somebody else came into the ladies.

Later, in a corner of the hotel car park, she could see her mother confronting her father. She could not hear exactly what they were saying but there were voices raised in anger. As she expected, her father was showing no signs of regret, remorse or concern.

There was palpable tension in the car on the journey back to Paddy's house. Josey sat stiff and red-eyed, and Nuala could sense Dan's resentment towards herself for complaining. If Paddy was aware of an 'atmosphere' he gave no sign, and chatted amiably to Dan about the weather and hay-making.

Back at Paddy's farm, Dan glowered at his daughter and beckoned her to one side in a secluded leafy spot down the avenue near the garage. The others were on their way into the house.

'Come here to me, you,' he hissed at her.

When she was within close enough range to smell the whiskey

fumes from his breath, he drew out his hand and slapped her hard across the face. He put all his strength into the blow. The stinging pain, the humiliation of a slap in the face – she had been through it all before, but she would never get used to it. She didn't want to cry but the tears came in floods. She had that familiar buzzing, throbbing sensation in her head that always followed a blow.

'If there's one thing I can't stand it's ingratitude,' said Dan. 'You've been upsetting me and Mammy again after all we've done for you. And every time you do that you know what's going to happen – you're in for a slap. Do you understand that?'

'Yes, Daddy.'

'Now, I don't want any more complaints, right? You're a married woman now and you do what he tells you to do. He's your husband and he can do what he wants, right?'

'Yes, Daddy.'

The message was clear – Paddy can rape you if he wants to, and you'd just better get to like it.

'Now stop that whingeing. Don't get me annoyed again.'

Nuala tried to stifle her tears as best she could as she walked with her father back to the house.

On the way, he paused and looked at his daughter with a kind of hurt look. 'Do you realise all I have done for you? I've got you a catch that other girls would die for. Just look at the big house you're living in now. Just look at all them acres. Fellas like that aren't ten a penny. They're hard to find. Isn't it a lot better than being married to some gobshite in a council cottage? And what thanks have I got for it? After all the running around I've done, all I hear about are petty complaints. It would be really nice if certain people, not a million miles from here, could nod to me now and then and say, "Fair play to you, Daddy, and thanks for everything".'

'Yes, Daddy.'

Shortly after the rape, in an attempt to escape from the situation she was in, Nuala took a small overdose of aspirin. She knew it was not enough to cause death, but she reckoned she would be taken off to hospital where she could alert people to her plight. It would be a means of getting away from the house where she felt under constant threat.

She said to the husband, 'I'm after taking loads of tablets.' He drove her to the hospital himself. He didn't say much on the way. Her father was with them, giving out to her and lecturing her. She was pumped out in the general hospital and then transferred to another hospital for psychiatric tests. She told the nurses she had not really taken that many tablets at all, but that she just had to get away from that house. She was interviewed by a psychiatrist and he recorded everything she said on a tape recorder, although she did not realise at the time that he was taping the interview.

Later, she was called back into his office. She was shocked to see her father and the husband sitting there. The psychiatrist had this tape recorder on his desk. He confronted the two men, saying, 'Is this the real reason why this girl is here?' Then he began playing the tape of what she had said to him. Nuala was stunned. All she wanted to do was die. She was not expecting this. They had to sit there and listen to the full story, of how she had been forced into the marriage, how she had been raped by the husband, how she had been beaten. Looking back, she can't really blame the psychiatrist for doing it. After all, she had asked him for help, she had made serious allegations, and she supposed he had to check out what she was saying. When the tape was over, he looked at the two men and said, 'Well, is that true? Is that what really happened?'

Dan, being the smoother talker, did most of the explaining. He was very charming to the doctor, very polite, never lost his cool, and insisted that Nuala had told a complete pack of lies. Neither of them showed any anger in front of the psychiatrist. They were very clever. Dan was very convincing, and made out, as he always did in these situations, that Nuala was unstable, that she had a problem, and that unfortunately she was not to be believed. Nuala felt that the psychiatrist, even though he said very little, was wavering and beginning to wonder if she had told the full truth.

Every so often Dan would say to the husband, 'Isn't that lies, Paddy?' about some statement she had made and the husband would agree. They made out she had never been forced into any marriage, had never been raped, never been beaten. 'That never happened,' Dan would say. He had the 'cute hoor' trick of never admitting anything, of denying everything. Nuala was in shock, and can't remember exactly all they said, but they made out that she was very well treated, that they were doing their best for her, that she had everything she wanted and enjoyed a lady's life, and that she had very willingly married this man without any compulsion whatsoever, because she loved him. The husband just let Dan carry on. Paddy knew that Nuala had a lot of fear in her of her father. Seeing her father there with the husband, and fearing that the psychiatrist was doubting her story, Nuala caved in. She felt that they were winning and that she had lost out. She fell apart and did not stand up for herself.

Towards the end of his masterly apologia, Dan triumphantly delivered his *coup de grace*. He declared that Nuala had actually been brought into hospital wearing – he paused for dramatic effect – an expensive fur coat that had been bought for her by Paddy. That showed the depths of Paddy's generosity towards his young bride. How many other young married women in the county had been bought fur coats by their husbands? Could anyone tell him that? He was into his stride now, becoming more eloquent by the moment, like some backwoods barrister making his final pitch to the jury. 'All that I am telling you is facts!' he declared.

After a challenge by Dan, the psychiatrist asked a nurse to bring in the fur coat which had been lying on Nuala's hospital bed, and it was duly displayed in his office, like a make-or-break exhibit in a court case. Nuala at this stage was so demoralised that she could not tell the psychiatrist the real story about the fur coat. The garment had been given to Nuala's mother by a friend who didn't want it, and it had in turn been passed on by Josey to her daughter. Paddy had absolutely no hand, act or part in supplying the coat. Nuala was in floods of tears as the coat was brought in. She had given up the fight, feeling there was no point in going against her father and telling the true story.

Some days later Nuala was told that she was being sent home, and that her father and the husband were already at reception, waiting to collect her. She felt the shock of fear and despair. She knew she was going out to be beaten and abused. She was shouting and roaring at the hospital staff, 'You don't realise what's going to happen to me. I am going to be back here. I am going to be killed.' Then she ran out of her ward and into another ward. There were patients there sitting beside radiators. There were also nurses there and she said, 'If you try to send me home I am going through that window. I am not going with them. I am going to throw myself out.'

The nurses caught her and held her. She had got to know some of them. They were sympathetic towards her but there was nothing they could do to prevent her returning home. She was brought to the reception area. Through her tears, Nuala swore at her husband and her father, shouting, 'I don't fucking well want to go with you.' The nurses talked gently to her and calmed her down, and persuaded her it would be best for her to go quietly with the two men who had called to collect her. Nuala went quietly in the end. The two men put her into the husband's car and set off on the journey to Paddy's house. They gave her the silent treatment for quite some time. They were talking to each other as they travelled along but neither said anything to Nuala. Then, when they were a safe few miles away from the hospital, it happened. Dan, who had a heavy ring on his finger, turned and hit his daughter a punch, full-force into her face, with his ring. He split her lip and she was pumping blood.

Nuala was in a private hospital for a gynaecological operation at one stage around this period. When she returned home, the orders from her father and from Paddy were that she was to sleep with the husband in his bed. The very idea made her skin crawl, but the alternative would have been constant beatings from her father, and she felt she had no choice. The husband had his way with her: it was rape as far as she was concerned. Her father had brainwashed her, 'If you play your cards right, he won't live long and you will get the house and the farm.' Dan threatened her that if she did not do as she was told she would be beaten to within an inch of her life. He would say to her, 'You have a lovely house here, everything you want, so just do as you are fucking told. He can do whatever he wants.' He would say this over and over again. She gave up. She knew the husband was going to have sex with her one way or another so she might as well lie down and take it. She felt under extreme pressure, and it was the easiest option.

In the following months every time Paddy went to have sex with her, she told him, 'Please don't. I don't want to do this. I hate you for what you are doing to me,' but he never listened. Sometimes she would wail, like a child, 'I want to go home to my Mammy.' But these pleas fell on deaf ears. Paddy would have sex with her about twice a week. She hated and dreaded these encounters. She gave in because it was easier than being tied down like an animal or being beaten up. Even though the law of the land at that time did not recognise rape within marriage, Nuala considers every act of intercourse with her husband to have been rape from a moral point of view, because it was done against her will, and under duress.

After some time, she decided she could not take it any more. She had spotted a bottle with a dose for cattle that was labelled 'lethal to humans'. She hoped that this would knock her out – forever. She was in the sitting room, just off the kitchen, when she opened the bottle, put it to her lips and drank the contents. She thought that Sylvester was up the fields but in fact he was in the kitchen and saw her, through a glass door, drinking the lethal liquid. He guessed what it was and immediately alerted Paddy and showed him what she had taken. Paddy phoned her parents who drove to the house straight away. She remained conscious as parents, husband and workman huddled around her. Somebody made up a foul-tasting mixture and her father forced it down her throat to make her vomit. She was ill for weeks afterwards. Whatever it was she drank seemed to take the lining off her insides. She suffered badly, and found it very hard to eat or drink.

After the first rape, she knew that all this talk of a 'no sex' marriage was just a sham. She wondered if her father or the husband had ever been really serious about it. She began to think it had just been a confidence trick by the two of them to lure her into this marriage that was steadily destroying her. Even if there was a legal document guaranteeing there would be 'no physical contact' in this relationship, how could it be enforced if Paddy decided to break the agreement? She knew that any protests on her part to Paddy or her father would be ignored. She was descending into a dark pit of despair. Could it really get any worse? Once she pleaded with her father, 'I want to go home, Daddy. I'll be a good girl. I won't do anything wrong. Please, Daddy, please.'

As time went by, she came to understand her father's strategy. Dan wanted her to have as much sex as possible with Paddy, in the hope that the shock of making love with a lively, attractive young teenager more than forty-five years his junior would kill him off. Then the really big prize would be won – an extremely valuable house and farm. She came to realise that her father's plan was that this wealth would then be shared with the rest of the family. They were not involved in the conspiracy, of course, and the scheme was the sole brainchild of her father. Her view is that her father, because of serious lung problems, knew that he did not have very long to live, and that part of his motivation in marrying her off to Paddy was to try to secure the financial future of his family by grabbing a valuable property. Unfortunately for her, she just happened to be the sacrificial victim, a means to an end. Dan's immediate 'cut', the Morris Mini and the £2,500, was simply a prelude to a much bigger bonanza, if Dan could survive long enough. Nuala believed that despite all Dan's bonhomie towards Paddy, he really wanted to see the farmer just go away and die as quickly as possible. She guessed that if the husband had died first, her father would have moved into his house. Dan often said it was his dream to live in a big house. Nuala's previous boyfriend Larry lived in a big old family house that he was going to inherit, and she reckoned that this had been a major factor in making Larry acceptable in Dan's eyes. The relationship with Paddy had more to offer in material terms. Paddy was the goose that laid the golden egg, and on this occasion at least, killing the golden goose made sense, and sex might just do the trick.

CHAPTER EIGHT

THE BEATINGS

Nuala and her mother got off the bus and walked up the avenue to Paddy's house. It was some time after the first rape. Nuala noticed a silence, and she began to feel uneasy. Whenever she approached the house she could always be sure of a welcome from Lassie. The sheepdog would detect her from way off and come bounding along the avenue to greet her, yelping out a welcome. But today there was no sign of Lassie.

Nuala saw Sylvester standing in front of the house. He was in tears and shaking. The workman said, 'Oh Nuala, you are going to be crying in a minute.' Nuala began to panic. 'What's wrong, Sylvester? Where's Lassie?'

The workman, too upset to talk, led the way to a stable, opened the half-door, and there, hanging by a rope from the rafters, was the lifeless body of the sheepdog. Lassie's eyes, which had so often lit up with affection for Nuala, were now wide open in death, the look of terror still in them. 'He's after killing Lassie,' said Sylvester hoarsely.

Paddy had strung up Lassie to die slowly by strangulation. He never said why he did it. Nuala broke down and wept with shock and grief, holding the body of her beloved Lassie tightly in her arms. She knew the dog's only offence was loving her. She felt she knew exactly the message the husband was sending to her. He had seen her giving so much love and affection to the dog and he wanted her to give the same to him. By hanging the unfortunate animal, he was saying to her, 'Now, you have no-one to love. You will have to love me.'

She was roaring crying over the dog and the husband was standing there in the background, laughing. She had noticed him in the farm-yard, looking on and grinning, as Sylvester took her to the stable where Lassie's body was hanging. As Nuala shrieked, Paddy chuckled all the more. Nuala's mother was with her and she was aghast, speechless. At one stage Nuala said to her, 'I wish I was that dog.' She kept cuddling the dog and Sylvester had to pull her away before cut-ting down the animal for burial. The incident brought home to her just how much she hated Paddy. She felt that if somebody had handed her a gun at that moment she would have blown him to pieces.

Just as Paddy's son had predicted, it was not long before the farmer became violent towards his young bride. Nuala was thrashed for tak-ing an unauthorised trip to town. She had been bored and feeling like a prisoner. She just wanted to get out of the house and see some bright lights – a natural urge for any teenager. There was a bus route that passed by the big gates at the end of the avenue from the house, and after saving up some money she got on the bus and went to the local big town for the day – without Paddy's permission. Suicide was al-ways on her mind, and she thought she would have one last big 'blo-wout' before she died. She went on a pub crawl in two different towns, visiting a range of pubs. She got so drunk that she cannot to this day remember how she got home.

She remembers knocking at the door late at night, then the husband opening the door, a look of fury on his face. She heard the words 'Nobody does this to me', and then a fist came swinging towards her face. He was a strong man who could throw a heavy punch. She only felt the first blow. She experienced pain and shock as the fist connected, fol-lowed by an explosion of light, and then nothingness. She woke up at dawn on the floor of the hallway, bloodstained and bruised, her lips thick from the blows, and with injuries to her nose. She had lain there all night, out cold. 'Oh my God,' she groaned. 'I'm marked all over.' She stumbled out the door and made her way to the nearest house, which was the local presbytery. Father McMichael, Paddy's parish priest, lived there. The priest's housekeeper gave her first aid, bathed her wounds, and walked with her back to Paddy's house. It was to be the first of many beatings.

Nuala had turned to drink as a way of blotting out her agony. From an early age she knew about alcohol and about the way it could alter your mood. She had often seen her father go out in the morning sober and come home roaring drunk, and she thought it was a way to evade reality, a kind of anaesthetic for the pain of living. She hoped that, with drink, if the husband beat her up she wouldn't feel it, if he raped her she wouldn't feel it. She noticed that Paddy kept a bottle of whiskey locked in a cupboard in the sitting room. Farmers with whom he was doing a deal would sometimes call to the house and Paddy would take out the bottle and give the guest a drink. Nuala kept watch and discovered where the key was kept. She began to 'raid' the cupboard from time to time to take a quick slug from the bottle.

To cover her tracks, she filled up the bottle with black tea. She thought it was safe enough to do this as Paddy's preferred tipple was brandy. There came a time when the liquid in the whiskey bottle was almost totally black tea. And then, to her shock, the inevitable happened. A farmer was invited into the house one day and was offered a glass of whiskey by Paddy. Nuala was with Paddy in the sitting room and she was on tenterhooks as the farmer put the glass to his lips. She managed to catch his eye and gave him the most grovelling, supplicatory look she could summon up.

Nuala kept looking at him pleadingly, imploring him, 'Please don't tell.' If he had said something, she was in for a hiding. She breathed a silent prayer of thanks to God when the farmer picked up the message. He suddenly understood what was going on. He said, 'That's a grand drop of whiskey, Paddy.' She said below her breath, 'Fair play to you for protecting me.' Whenever she met him in the pub or the village afterwards, he would grin and say to her, 'That was a grand drop of tea, Nuala!'

One of the offences that would merit a beating from Paddy was getting drunk – and she loved to get drunk now as a temporary escape from reality. Sometimes the supply of drink in the house ran out, and Paddy would not be in a hurry to buy more. Often, Nuala would not be in a position to go out on her own to the pub, so she would talk Paddy into taking her out for a drink. She would put on an act of being nice to him to get her way. She would turn on the charm, smile at him and put her arm around him. She knew she was being devious but it was a matter of survival. Mostly, he didn't mind bringing her to a pub, as it was a chance to show her off.

They would go to one of a number of bars which Paddy liked to visit, and he would usually buy Nuala a half pint of Harp lager. For her, this was just an appetiser, and she would try to get more drink without him knowing. A pub usually had more than one counter, or a snug, and she would pretend to make frequent visits to the ladies, using the opportunity to knock back booze out of sight of her husband. The goal was to get drunk without Paddy noticing that she was drunk. Sometimes other men, intrigued by this beautiful young teenager, would buy her drink. Occasionally she had far too much to drink, and it showed, and Paddy would fly into a rage.

One night she was in the toilets of a particular pub after really hitting the booze. She knew she was becoming quite seriously inebriated. She remarked to a girl about her own age who approached her in the toilet, 'I'm pissed. I'm in for a hiding tonight from the oul' fella.' The girl said, 'Why don't you smoke a bit of this? He won't be able to smell it and you'll be grand.' This was Nuala's introduction to cannabis, which in the mid-1970s was only gradually making inroads into rural Ireland. The drug was more common in the big towns and cities, where it had been making its presence felt since the late 1960s.

Gradually, the girl introduced Nuala to the local suppliers. These were lads in their late teens or early twenties, some unemployed, others in dead-end jobs, and all from the 'wrong side of the tracks'. Dealing in illegal drugs, albeit soft drugs, was not only profitable – it seemed to bring a frisson of drama and danger and perhaps even glamour into small-town lives that were otherwise drab and boring. Some of these lads would hang around the pubs, but of course the publicans never realised they were drug dealers. Most people in rural Ireland at that time knew hardly anything about drugs. The dealers were tearaways, young men inclined towards petty crime. Locally, they were called 'the rough crowd', and Nuala would notice that there would be nobody else sitting with them in the pubs.

Very soon, Nuala was a regular client of the pushers. She was getting to know 'the rough crowd', entering the furtive world of these young 'outsiders' of her own youthful generation who were part of an underground Ireland of the 1970s. She would somehow manage to get the money for drugs – although sometimes the dealers would give her cannabis free. Enough hash for a joint was about £2 – a lot of money in those days. But Nuala found that if she was careful she would get a couple of days out of it. The joints she rolled were huge. She would smoke at home in the toilet, or out on the farm or up in the haybarn. In the beginning, she would take two pulls from a joint and she was gone – she would be on a high. The husband could not understand it. He would be giving out to her and she would be giggling and laughing. He never found out what made her like that. He suspected she was on something, but didn't have a clue what it was. His generation knew nothing about drugs.

Smoking cannabis helped her to forget. Once, on a high after a joint, she came into the house and threw her arms around Paddy and said, 'I love you.' He was astounded, and could not believe what he was hearing. Looking back on it now, she reckons that there must have been some really potent stuff in that particular joint.

She used to meet the pushers in different places, in pubs or outside the shops in Dunkellin village or behind the church. Anywhere at all. In addition to smoking joints, she also smoked cigarettes. After a time, the husband didn't mind her puffing cigarettes too much as he smoked himself, but he would seldom give her one. If she had no cigarettes of her own, she would mostly have to do without them. Sylvester used to smoke so she would get the odd one from him and give him some too. Nuala noticed that Paddy would just buy packets of ten – she never saw him buy twenty. She thought that was really mean.

To finance her growing taste in drink and drugs, Nuala needed money. She got a certain amount from her husband, but she also began to sell off possessions to fund her drink-drugs habit. She was very proud of one outfit she had, a white leather jacket and matching miniskirt. It was the height of fashion. She knew she was the only girl in the whole area to have an outfit like that. But so eager was she to get money for drugs that she secretly sold off her treasured outfit to a girl in a pub.

Sometimes, under the influence of drink, she would stand up to the husband, but she was not physically strong enough for him and he would sometimes end up beating her. She would say to him, 'I will kill you, you bastard,' and tell him she hated him from the day she met him. She reckoned that once he got what he wanted from her as regards sex he did not care if she loved him or not. She would cry into his face and say, 'Please don't do this to me. I hate you,' but she reckoned it was just part of living to him. He did not seem to care in the slightest. If she said she did not want to have sex with him, he would just have it anyway. He would beat her down and force her. Sometimes he would beat her both before and during sex. Nuala felt that she was dealing with a sadist, and that the more he saw her upset the greater the kick he got out of it. She could see it in his face.

As Nuala became drawn into the murky world of drugs, she discovered that there was something else that she could get from the black market through one of the 'rough crowd' – sleeping pills. She doesn't know how she would have survived without these sedatives. She reckons that buying the pills was one of the best investments she made at this period – it was really money well spent, and the pills greatly enhanced the quality of her life. The pills were not for herself but for slipping a 'Mickey Finn' to the husband without his knowledge. Despite his years, Paddy was a fit, virile man, and in an attempt to get some respite from his sexual advances, she began secretly dosing his food with the tablets, which she would laboriously crush up into powder form with a fork. It was hard work preparing the Mickey Finn but it was worth it. He would sleep like a baby after eating a meal or having a bowl of soup laced with sedatives. If she could knock him out early in the night, she would even slip out of the house and go to a pub by herself or even to a dance in Dunkellin village, which was, of course, within walking distance. It wasn't with the idea of meeting other men – she had had her fill of men at this stage. It was simply to get out of the house, to sense some freedom and above all to get more drink.

She would give Paddy soup with the sedatives in it, and she would then get ready to go out. By the time she would be ready, he would have conked out. To make sure that Paddy was fast asleep, she would clump noisily up and down the stairs and make a racket, and if he still slumbered on, she knew the Mickey Finn was working and that all was well, thank God. There were times when she would leave the house wearing jeans but with a skirt hidden under her sweater. She would then take off the jeans and hide them under a stile beside the big iron gates at the end of the drive, and put them back on on her way home. Wearing jeans was less of a sign that she had been out on the town. The problem was, sometimes she would stagger home so drunk that she would forget about the jeans, and leave them under the stile. But mostly it didn't matter anyway, because Paddy would still be fast asleep in the chair when she returned. She would have to wake him up as best she could, and then she and Sylvester would drag him up the stairs to the bedroom. Paddy would be only semi-conscious as he changed into his night clothes and went to bed.

Sylvester also benefited from the sleeping pills trick, although Nuala never told him about the tablets in case he would blurt it out. Despite the fact that Sylvester was not allowed into the house beyond the kitchen without special permission from Paddy, Nuala would give him the freedom of the establishment when the boss was knocked out after being dosed with the pills. Sylvester normally had to wash at a sink in the kitchen and use the outside toilet, but when she would get Paddy's back turned she would let Sylvester into the house, let him use the bathroom and feed him properly. Whenever she got the chance she would give the workman a hot meal, whatever was available – unless she had it doped. There were nights when she would have no money to go out drinking, then the husband would be upstairs in bed snoring his brains out because of the tablets while Sylvester would be lying back in the sitting room in front of a roaring fire, chatting and laughing and watching the telly with Nuala.

Sometimes Paddy would be away at meetings of the Irish Farmers Association or playing cards. She would seize on these opportunities also to take a break from the tedium of life in the big, melancholy old house. If she went to a pub, she would usually just sit by herself and drink, although there were men who would send her over drink. There were risks involved. It was a small community, and word would sometimes get back to Paddy that Nuala had been out on the town. She knew then that she would be in for a hiding. She knew that men would not betray her but there were some local women who hated her guts and who would be fully capable of squealing on her. She felt there were women who despised her because the men would be talking about her and saying, 'She's a fine bit of stuff.' The men would buy her lollipops and sweets if she went into a shop, or drink if she went into a pub. Some of the women resented the attention she was getting. Walking down the street, she felt they just wanted to choke her. If she thought they were watching, she'd put on an act and wiggle her bum, just to annoy them even more.

As Paddy clouted her he would be interrogating her: 'Were you with another man? Were you?' She came to be wary about what Sylvester, in his innocence, would let slip to Paddy. Sylvester would come in and say, 'I met so-and-so down the village and he says he fancies Nuala.' Or he might say, 'I saw some fella watching Nuala.' Of course the husband would blame her for all of this. She had to drum it into Sylvester that there were some things he shouldn't say because he would get her into trouble. Sometimes, to impress on Sylvester the importance of not blowing the gaff, she would give him small cash gifts, which to him were like a fortune. 'There's a few bob for you, Sylvester – now keep your mouth shut!'

CHAPTER NINE

THE POLICE

Nuala went into a shop one day to buy some cigarettes. She smoked one to calm her nerves. She didn't know anybody in this big town. She stood on the footpath outside the shop, puffing at the cigarette, looking idly at the traffic thundering by, glancing now and then at the steps leading up to the entrance to the garda station. She wondered if she was doing the right thing in going to the police. In the past, she had never had much to do with 'the law'. She was wary of the guards and was very uptight about what might lie in store for her in the station. When she had sucked the last dose of consoling nicotine from the cigarette, she flicked it away and walked slowly up the steps.

Some time after her husband began to rape and beat her, Nuala made what was, for her, a momentous decision – she was going to complain to the gardaí. She would tell the police authorities exactly how her husband had raped her, and ask them to take action. She would also report her husband and her father for their physical violence against her. She wasn't clear in her own mind what she wanted the authorities to do. She wasn't sure whether she wanted her two tormentors to be cautioned, or brought to court, or fined, or jailed. She just wanted some action taken that would stop them oppressing her.

She knew little about the law of the land, and in her innocence was not even familiar with the word 'rape'. All she had was a profound conviction that what her husband had done to her was wrong. Surely the authorities would have to do something about it? Surely Ireland had laws, and surely she was entitled to the protection of those laws? Her father and her husband had made the most fundamental decisions about her future and had not even bothered to consult her. But surely, at the end of the day, they were not above the law, even though they acted as if they were? Nuala was aware of the gardaí arresting some of the youths from 'the rough crowd' in her own home area for a variety of petty offences. She reasoned that if gardaí were enforcing the law and penalising young people, surely they should also enforce it to protect a young person? Surely it had to be a two-way street? Surely the law was there not just to punish young people but to safeguard them as well?

Reporting her father and her husband to the gardaí was a daunting decision for any teenage girl, and it was one she had to make totally by herself. In Paddy's district, there was nobody who could advise her, nobody in whom she could confide. She was an outsider in that community, something of a freak, and she knew how deeply some of the local women despised her. She had lost contact with many of her own teenage girlfriends in her home district seven miles away. There was still a great bond between herself and her friend Carmel but it was difficult to keep in touch. Some of her friends tended to avoid her because they really did not know what to say to her now that she was a married woman while they were still at school. Anyway, seven miles was quite a distance if you did not have a car or a bicycle – the buses did not run that often. Keeping in touch by phone wasn't really a viable option either. Many people in rural Ireland in that era, including Nuala's own family, did not have a phone. When she or Paddy wanted to contact her parents, they had to phone a neighbour's house. Making unsupervised calls from Paddy's house was difficult, in view of the fact that he locked the phone away when he went out. The end result was that when she finally went to the authorities with her complaints she had nobody to back her up and give her moral support or guidance. In those days there was no such thing as a Rape Crisis Centre in her region, and if there were homes for battered wives, she was unaware of them.

One day she decided that the moment of truth had come, and that she would make her move – she would call in the forces of the state. She told Paddy she was getting the bus to see her mother. Trips like this were permitted. However, on this occasion, she stayed on the bus as it went through her mother's village of Knockslattery and continued on to the nearest big town.

She went to the gardaí out of fear. She had just turned seventeen. She was terrified of the rapes that had occurred and was also terrified of what was going to happen in the future. As she went into the garda station she really wanted to speak to a woman, and if there had been a female garda there she would have gone straight to her. She did not see any women, only men. There was a garda behind the counter, and a couple of others in the background, doing different things.

She could sense them sizing her up. There was this reserve that cops had, it was a male thing, probably the same all over the world. They didn't want to let their guard down. They met all types. They had to deal with the dregs of society. They had to keep their distance, not get too close; they couldn't get emotionally involved. The garda behind the counter nodded to her politely, looking at her quizzically.

'I want to report something,' she said.

She gave her name and address, and paused, trying to work out how best to express herself.

'I was forced, against my will, to have sex.'

The garda's eyes opened wide. He was fully on the alert now. Nuala realised she also had the full attention of the two gardaí in the background.

'You are saying that you were raped?'

It was a word that she was not very familiar with, but now that he said it she knew she had heard it before. It sounded like the right word.

'Yes,' she replied.

'Who did this to you?'

'A man called Paddy McGorril.'

'But that's your surname. Is he related?'

'He's my husband.'

The young garda shook his head and put down his pen. 'If it was your husband, Nuala, you were not raped, at least not in terms of the law.'

'You mean he can do this to me any time he likes? Surely that can't be right. I'm afraid of what he might do to me in the future. And I am also afraid of what I might do to him.'

'We have to work within the law, Nuala. And Irish law does not recognise rape within marriage.'

'He's an elderly man. I was forced to marry him. And they said I would not have to sleep with him. And now this happens. You have to help me.'

'Nuala, with the best will in the world, what can we do? We can't charge your husband with rape.'

Oh God, that was just what she was expecting. She was a fool even to think the law could do anything for her. The law was framed by big shots for big shots. What did the politicians in the Dáil know about the problems of little people like her?

'He beat me and so did my father, who forced me to marry him. The two of them cut my face and left me black and blue. Surely you can do something about that?' There was an edge of annoyance and frustration coming into her voice.

'I don't see any marks now.'

'The marks have gone.'

'It would have been a help if you had come to us straight away, when you still had the marks of the beatings. Otherwise, without witnesses, it can come down to your word against theirs.'

She turned on her heel and stormed out. She was in tears as she walked down the steps. She felt more vulnerable, more desolate, more alone than ever. The gardaí had been her last resort. They were there to protect people but they could do nothing to stop her being raped. For her, this was the last straw as far as the civil authorities were concerned. Okay, the gardaí did not make the laws, but in her emotional state she lumped them all together – guards, politicians, the lot. She felt embittered against the whole pack of them, against every organ of the state. She became totally rebellious against Irish society. If she heard of a robbery being carried out, she'd pray the robbers were never caught, and if a garda or an RUC man in the North got shot, she'd say the bastards deserved it. She began to have sympathy with the rebels in society.

In all this despair, she was grateful for one small mercy – neither her father nor her husband ever discovered that she had reported them to the gardaí. Since they were not going to be charged with anything, the consequences for her if they had found out did not bear thinking about.

If the state could not help her, she wondered if the church would come to her aid. But she didn't fare much better when she went to see a priest, now dead, who lived in another part of the county. She was on one of her rare day trips away from home at the time.

She was drunk that day. She saw the presbytery – that was a place where people could get help, wasn't it? She was in a daze, and still can't remember everything clearly. She remembers being shown into the parlour by the housekeeper. She dozed off or passed out and awoke with shock to find an elderly priest leaning over her, pawing at her. Her panties had been pulled down. She became hysterical. He told her to shut up. She was crying. She heard the door opening. The housekeeper walked in. The priest left the room. Nuala is convinced that the sound of the housekeeper opening the door saved her from a worse fate.

All Nuala wanted to do was to get out of that house. She said to the housekeeper, 'That priest, he tried to do something dirty to me.'

The housekeeper flew into a rage. 'How dare you say that about a man of God! You are a liar. You are evil.'

Nuala could not believe a priest would behave like this. In the Ireland of the time, stories of errant clerics just did not surface in the media. It was only in recent years, with all the court cases and news stories to do with clerical sex abuse cases, that Nuala began to see her own experience in context. The stark reality was that there was a minority of priests who abused quite a number of victims. To this confused teenager back in the 1970s, there seemed to be nobody in the whole wide world who could come to her aid. The combined forces of church and state seemed unable to do anything for her.

One day her husband's parish priest, Father McMichael, called around to see her. She could see his house across the fields. Paddy wanted his wife to fulfil her religious duties and would sometimes order her to get down on her knees and say her prayers. He would also scold her for not going to Mass. In the rural Ireland of the time, almost every Catholic attended Sunday Mass. Paddy himself was a regular participant in the sacraments and Nuala found this display of piety rather odd when she considered how he raped and beat her.

Fr McMichael was now calling around to see if he could get her back to church. As far as Nuala was concerned, she did not want to know anything about the Catholic Church. It was in a church that she became locked into this awful marriage with no hope of escape, and it was in a church that she was shown off like some kind of trophy by the sadist to whom she was sold. And then, when she looked for help from a priest, he had tried to molest her. She had had her fill of organised religion, even though she retained a belief in God and would pray to him and talk to him in her own way from time to time. But she dreaded the thought of going into a church, and even passing by a church almost made her physically sick.

'Good morning, Nuala,' said Fr McMichael as she opened the front door to his knock.

'He's not here, Father. He's gone to the creamery.'

'Oh it's not himself I called to see, Nuala.'

She wondered to herself, 'Oh Jaysus, what's the problem now? Just one bloody thing after another.'

'Come in, Father.'

She didn't really feel like the mistress of the house. Even though she liked to keep the place tidy she could not take real pride in this big house. Swanning around the place did not boost her ego in the slightest. She showed the priest into the sitting room.

The priest was ill at ease. He coughed loudly after sitting down, as if he was building up to what he had to say.

Nuala sat awkwardly on the edge of a chair facing him. She wasn't really good at making small talk with parish priests.

'I haven't seen you for a while, Nuala.'

'Well, I've been here all the time, Father. I haven't gone away, you know.'

'I mean I haven't seen you at Mass.'

'Well, that's not surprising, Father, since I have not been going.' She hadn't meant to be cheeky. It just kind of slipped out.

'Sure maybe you go sometimes in your own family parish?'

'No, I haven't been going at all.'

The priest cleared his throat again. 'Now, Nuala, you know it's a mortal sin to miss Mass on a Sunday. Paddy is worried about it.'

'Oh, was he talking to you about me?'

'Well, it kinda came up in conversation, like. I thought I might have a word with you.'

'Well, it's like this, Father,' she told the priest, 'I don't want to go to Mass.'

'But why, Nuala? Sure isn't it the centrepiece of our religion?'

'I hate it. You can't make me go, so I'm not going.' She did not really want to spell out to him how she felt embarrassed at being paraded in front of all these gawping parishioners. Talking about it just added to the embarrassment.

'You will never get to heaven, Nuala, if you go on like this.'

'I don't give a shite. Sure there isn't a heaven anyway.' She was becoming more impatient now, and didn't care if she was being cheeky or not.

'You will go to hell, Nuala, if you are not careful.'

'May I correct you, Father? I'm in hell already, living here with this galoot. It's ye fuckers who are going to hell.'

When she made the latter comment, she was thinking primarily of the priest who had tried to molest her. Fr McMichael looked shocked.

She guessed that Fr McMichael and many of the locals knew that she had been forced into this marriage. She told him now that the church had been of little help to her. She was really impertinent towards him that day. Fr McMichael had had an injury to his throat years before. The rumour was that he had been shot. As a result, he could not speak clearly. At one point she said to him impatiently, 'I can't even understand what you're saying.' At this stage, she just did not care. She had turned against the church, against society, against everyone. Each day she got up out of bed she was more bitter, more full of hurt, more full of hate. Especially towards men. The priest was absolutely shocked when she talked to him like that, and he never came near her afterwards. The priest told the husband what she had said and the husband told her father. She got a beating from the husband that day, and that night she got another beating from her father because of the way she had talked to the parish priest.

There was a kind of ritual attached to the beatings administered by Paddy. Usually he would grab her from behind and he would inform her why he was beating her. When he was clouting her for giving cheek to the parish priest he was saying, 'How dare you talk to the parish priest like that, and me a figure of society!' Nuala was intrigued by his use of that phrase, 'a figure of society'. Who did he think he was?

Nuala considered that Paddy was always trying to put her down. His attitude was that she had married into his big farm and that she was beneath him socially. He used to tell her that she was nothing and that she came from nothing. He said she should be down on her knees thanking God for what she had. Once she was lying on the floor after he had knocked her down, and he put his foot on her and said, 'You are dirt. You are beneath me and beneath me you will stay.' Nuala hit back with the traditional Irish catch-all, all-purpose retort to a personal slight, 'That's what you think!'

Sometimes when he was hitting her, or if she was being difficult and he wanted to belittle her, he would say, 'You're mine, you bitch. I bought you. Do you realise how much I paid for you? I own you.'

She is grateful at least for one small mercy – Paddy never used a weapon to beat her with, such as a stick. The beatings with his hands were bad enough, but she reckons that if a weapon had been used it would have been far worse. He usually hit her with his clenched fist, and her eyes were a favourite target. She also ended up with her forehead split, and she still bears a mark on her chin from a beating. Once she had to stay in bed for two days after a particularly vicious assault. Sometimes she would cry when she was beaten, but she became tougher as time went on, and would do her best not to weep, so as not to give her husband the satisfaction of seeing her in tears. In the end, she didn't cry, she wouldn't cry.

Many's the time she was sporting black eyes. She used to wear dark glasses going outside the house to hide the bruises around her eyes. She would wear them out of shame, even though it might be a winter's day. The problem was, you could not totally conceal bruises with dark glasses. She would wear them on the bus going to see her mother, and on one occasion her father was furious with her for travelling on a bus while she had visible injuries. 'What did you get on that feckin' bus for? Everybody will be talking.' Of course he wasn't angry with the person who had actually caused the injuries.

She used to hear them whispering on the bus, 'That's the one that's married to the oul' fella.' Once she turned around to these people who were gossiping and said, 'That's right, that's me, why don't you say it out loud!' They got the shock of their lives. She can't remember where she got the glasses – they were an old cheap pair. Charley, the bus driver, was a nice man and he often saw her with bruises. He knew what was happening. He took pity on her and gave her a better pair of dark glasses, with gold rims.

There were other times when Nuala would go down to Dunkellin village with her visible injuries to show them off, as a way of exposing what was being done to her, and shaming those responsible. If she had bruises on her arms, she would wear a short-sleeved top to exhibit them, and if she had bruises to her face, she would not try to disguise them. Then they got clever, her father and the husband. They would hit her on the body where the marks would not show. They mostly left her face alone after a while. The marks would be too obvious.

Sometimes, the husband would beat her for some transgression, and he would then take her to her father's house, and the father would beat her again for the same offence. Paddy would not tell her father he had beaten her. She would sob to her father as he began to hit her, 'He's already after doing that.' The husband would say, 'I didn't touch you.' Her father would say, 'You deserve every slap you get.' There were times when the two of them beat her together, like sadism in stereo. She would be belted around the place, both in her father's house and in the husband's house.

Sometimes a beating came about as a result of some quite unpredictable incident. One such incident occurred during an election. Nuala received a voting card, and was mystified as to how her name got on the voters' register, as she was still below the legal voting age. The husband, like her father, was a great Fianna Fáil supporter. She went down with the husband to the polling station. She supposed he saw her as another vote for the party. When she went in, she told an official what age she was, and he said she could not vote. He thanked her for telling him. She got a thrill out of doing it. The husband was outraged. When he got her outside, he said, 'Why the hell did you do that? Why didn't you just go in and vote like everybody else?' She got a beating from him later for that. And then he brought her to her father's house, told him what she had done, and her father gave her a beating as well.

Dan was strongly republican, and would canvass for Fianna Fáil in elections. He would stand at the gate of the polling station on the day of the voting with the party workers, giving out leaflets. That was always a big day, and he would take the day off from work. It was like a Holy Day. The husband wouldn't do much work that day either. Of course Dan knew that when the voting was over there would be a big drinking session, with plenty of free drink. And when he would be out canvassing, he would be looking to make a sale for his business as well. He never missed a chance.

Since nobody would help her escape from this nightmare world of violence and rape, Nuala was tempted to take the law into her own hands. Paddy was looking out a window on the top storey of the house one day and she was standing behind him. She was tempted to grab him by the legs and heave him out. The fall would almost certainly have killed him. The window was only slightly open and she tried to open it more, but it was stuck. Every other time she had been able to open it easily. Despite the temptation, she probably would not have shoved him out. She had this odd feeling that he guessed the thought that had crossed her mind. He turned around, gave her a strange, quizzical look – and never put his head out that window again.

There were times, especially when she was being beaten, that she threatened that she would kill him. Remembering the first rape, she told him several times, 'If you ever tie me down again, I will kill you. You had better watch your back.' He would look at her with contempt as if to say, 'That will never happen.' But he never did tie her down again. He might as well have done, because he raped her on many occasions. He was a very big man, much more physically powerful than her. By the time he had beaten her up she would be too weak to fight back, and would just surrender and give in. She would always stand up to him at first, but there was a limit to what she could achieve. And then, of course, there was always the intimidating thought of her father in the background.

Once, she was making Irish stew for the husband, and thought that, instead of sleeping pills, she would add in something a little stronger. She spooned in three large dollops of rat poison. Anybody who ate it would have had a terrible death. On reflection, she decided that she had gone just a little over the top, and dumped the lethal mix. Another time, she tried to put the husband out of action by knocking him off a ladder. He was up painting the upper part of the house when she distracted the attention of Sylvester who was holding the ladder by waving a fiver and telling him to come quickly. The unfortunate Sylvester forgot what he was doing, let go of the ladder and came over to investigate the fiver. The ladder promptly slid down, but Paddy only suffered a few bruises and the indignity of having paint splashed over him. The furious farmer sacked Sylvester and it was only after Nuala's entreaties that he was kept on. At times of desperation she went looking for Paddy's shotgun, but it was always locked away safely. She believes that had she got her hands on the weapon, she might have taken out both Paddy and her father.

Nuala liked to retreat into the room that she originally occupied before she was forced to sleep with the husband. The room was still a shrine to David Essex. Apart from the Essex posters adorning the walls, it was also where she kept her precious pop music magazines. She was in this room one day reading her magazines when Paddy strode in. She knew by his body language that there was going to be trouble.

He said to her, 'It's about time you stopped acting like a child. It's about time you grew up and began behaving like a married woman.'

With that, he began ripping down her posters and tearing them to shreds. Nuala screamed in horror and began to weep. Then he got her magazines and tore them up as well.

'I hate you, I hate you,' she screamed at him. He grinned with the satisfaction of knowing he had got to her.

He gathered up the ripped-up debris from the floor and carried it downstairs to throw into the fire. The distraught teenager followed him down, screaming, 'You bastard, I hate you. I hate you.'

Nuala had continued to jog regularly, mostly up and down the avenue. Sometimes Paddy would watch her going through her paces. She knew now she would never realise her dream of being a serious athlete, but jogging up and down the avenue was better than nothing. She didn't realise that there was somebody other than Paddy who observed her as she ran – a farmer in his thirties living in the area, who happened to see her as he passed along the road.

One night, when Nuala and her husband were in the pub, the young farmer said to Paddy, 'That girl you married, she has some body, some figure. I've seen her jogging down the avenue. I wouldn't have minded marrying her myself!' The young man meant it as a harmless compliment, but Paddy was furious. That night, when he got Nuala home, he laid into her with a beating, accusing her of flaunting herself in front of the farmer, and trying to attract him. Jealousy of the attentions of other men was always regarded as grounds for a beating in Paddy's paranoid world. Nuala's arms were black and blue after the thumping she got that night. The outcome was that she was forbidden to do any more running. She was heartbroken over the ban, but she found ways around it. When she was certain Paddy was going to be away for a few hours, she would put on her running gear and go jogging, making sure that Sylvester was sworn to silence.

After a time, Nuala noticed a sinister pattern to the beatings. Often, Paddy would follow up a thrashing by raping her. It was almost as if the two acts were expressions of his sense of power over her, a sense that was no doubt boosted by the knowledge that he had 'bought' her. Nuala figures that there was a sexual element in his violence, in his sadism. The violence could be unpredictable. He might come in from the farm in a bad humour and push her out of the way or give her a clout. Sometimes she would be so full of anger that she could not help saying things that would provoke him. This happened particularly when she was under the influence of drink. One cold winter's night when her parents were visiting the husband's house she took the opportunity to drop a really spectacular bombshell.

They were all gathered in the sitting room in front of the fire. Dan and Josey, the husband, and even Sylvester, were there. Nuala pitied Sylvester that night because it was freezing in the attic where he lived. She asked the husband's permission to bring him in. She had had a few drinks secretly that night, and now she was drinking what appeared to be black tea. But nobody realised it was laced with whiskey. Dan was asking the husband for a loan. Many a time the husband gave loans to her father, and she didn't believe he ever got the money back.

Dan had begun treating Paddy like a private bank.

Nuala was obsessed with the knowledge that her father had sold her for £2,500 and a car. She had heard the boasts often enough from the husband, especially when he was trying to belittle her. She had never challenged her father before about it. But on this particular night, under the influence of drink, she just felt like throwing it at him. When she heard her father asking the husband for a loan, she said to him, 'Didn't you get enough in the £2,500 and the Morris Mini?'

There was shock in the room. Nobody said anything for a moment. Nuala guessed that her father had warned Paddy that nobody, especially Nuala herself, must ever know about this transaction, that it had to be kept carefully under wraps. She could see the fury welling up in her father. He could have denied it but he didn't. After a long pause, he declared, 'How do you fucking well know about that?'

Nuala nodded towards her husband. 'He told me.'

To her satisfaction, Nuala had caused extreme embarrassment to the two men she hated most in her life. The strength of her father's reaction could be gauged by the fact that he had used a four-letter word in polite company. But she knew there would be a price to pay.

Paddy gave her a vicious beating that night for two transgressions – for being drunk, but above all for snitching on him and humiliating him in front of her parents.

And then, for good measure, he raped her.

CHAPTER TEN

THE PREGNANCY

Nuala's short life had been one long series of betrayals. Fate had betrayed her by giving her a father who was violent, cynical and ruthless. Her father had betrayed her by molesting her and then selling her off as a virtual sex slave. Her husband had betrayed her by breaking the 'no sex' promise and raping her. A priest had betrayed her by trying to sexually assault her when she came to him for help, when she was at her lowest ebb. The state had betrayed her by failing to have the laws and systems in place to come to her rescue after she was tied down and raped. And finally, her own body betrayed her ...

Nuala began getting sick in the mornings. She could not hold her food down. She could not understand what was going on in her body. This teenager who had never properly learned the facts of life talked to her mother, who informed her that she was probably pregnant. The news hit Nuala like a slap in the face. For most women at most times, it's marvellous to learn that they are expecting. But for Nuala, it was just disastrous. So far as she was concerned, this baby was the result of rape and she did not want it.

She asked her mother what was it like to be pregnant. Her mother replied soothingly, 'It's just like constipation.' Later, after a very difficult birth, she remarked grimly to her mother, 'Some constipation!'

She hated the feel of this foetus inside her, that had resulted from Paddy forcing himself upon her. She never willingly had sex with this man. She was either physically forced to have intercourse, or gave in because of intimidation. She could not bear the idea of having a baby that was conceived in these hideous circumstances. She felt her body had been invaded again.

She reasoned with herself that it was not the fault of the unfortunate baby. But she just could not bring herself to love this being that had been fathered by a man whom she hated and despised. She decided that she just did not want to live.

One day, in a hamfisted suicide attempt, she threw herself down the stairs. She was some months pregnant at the time. Because of the design of the stairs, she could not fall all the way. She launched herself from the landing halfway up and tumbled down. She landed at the bottom of the stairs. But she was only bruised and sore. Sylvester was in the kitchen and he heard her. He came and helped her up and brought her into the kitchen. She was sobbing, 'I can't even kill myself!' It seemed to her that she had nine lives.

Some time before this Nuala was on a bus that crashed. Three people were injured, and she was up in the front and unhurt. She said to the bus driver, 'Isn't it terrible that nothing happened to me!' He gave her this strange look. She could see he was saying to himself, 'What kind of headcase is this?'

She made another determined attempt to kill herself when she was more than five months pregnant. Paddy was away from the house at the time. She knew that her suicide would also mean death for her unborn baby. But she reasoned that she was not really setting out to kill the baby – only herself. Maybe, in any case, it was better for the two of them to bow out together, and not to have to face an appalling future. There were a lot of pills in the house – mostly medication for Paddy's late wife. Nuala swallowed a large and potentially lethal cocktail of pills and collapsed on the floor. Her mother had a key to the house and she happened to call around, and found Nuala. This probably saved the teenager's life, and that of her unborn baby. The distraught woman kept trying to wake up her daughter. Then Paddy came home. By now any hint of affection that he might have had for his wife early on in the marriage seems to have evaporated. Nuala later learned from her mother that as he looked at his wife lying on the ground, his embittered remark was, 'Let her die.' An ambulance was called and Nuala was taken to hospital.

A plainclothes garda came to see her. Ironically, he was from the station where she had gone to report the rape. He warned her sternly that it was against the law to commit suicide, and that she could be prosecuted for trying to kill herself. He looked very respectable in a heavy crombie overcoat and a hat. She resented being lectured by him. She could not help feeling cynical. There were no laws in place to prevent her being raped by her husband, but when she tried to escape from her misery, it was she, the victim, who got the warning from the cops. She felt there had to be something wrong with the system. Her experience helped to speed her evolution into a rebel who despised many aspects of Irish society.

Her father also called in. He had no sympathy. He wanted her out of the hospital and back with Paddy, where she belonged. He told her, 'I will kill you if you don't get out of here.' She was in the hospital for two or three weeks. It was during her stay in the hospital that she again told others of her plight. One person, neither a patient nor a staff member at the hospital, was particularly concerned, and felt that this was a scandal that should be exposed. This person decided to contact the *Sunday World*. I was the reporter given the details. At first, the story seemed hardly credible. After all, this was affluent, well-educated 1970s Ireland. We had just entered the European Common

Market. The era of arranged or enforced marriages was long since over – or was it?

The story seemed like something from the Middle Ages or some Third World banana republic, rather than from civilised, Christian Ireland. However, the informant seemed to be a very honest, concerned individual, not the type to be taken in by a tall story. And, by a curious twist of fate, I realised that I had previously come across the small businessman alleged to have sold off his daughter as a bride. Dan Slowney was described to me as a hard-drinking gambler with a reputation as a wheeler-dealer, somebody who, in Ireland, would be described as a 'cute hoor'. I had not met him, but had learned about him in the context of another story I had worked on during the previous year, and had seen him from a distance driving a ramshackle van. I had some contacts in Dan's neighbourhood, and was able to verify the broad outline of what I had been told by the informant.

Nuala was in her husband's car one Sunday, along with her parents, when one of the biggest bust-ups of her turbulent young life occurred. She had just been released from hospital where she had been treated after her suicide attempt. Her husband had picked up her parents after Mass and they were driving off on an outing – Nuala cannot remember exactly where. Paddy stopped the car outside the shop in Knockslattery and he and Dan went in to buy the Sunday newspapers. Her father could not read properly, but he would always buy the Sunday papers and carry them ostentatiously under his arm, as if to proclaim that he was fully literate. Whenever a letter arrived at the house for Dan, his wife would have to read it out for him. But Paddy could certainly read, and would buy national newspapers, the *Irish Press* and the *Irish Independent*, every day.

Nuala's father and her husband were standing beside the car, staring in shock at one of the newspapers. They were murmuring to each other. Every now and then they would glare at her. Then they got into the car and one of them flung a copy of the *Sunday World* at her. Nuala, who was in the front passenger seat, began to get very nervous, very uptight. What on earth was in the newspaper that had sparked off all this fury and resentment? Paddy began reading out loud from the article in the *Sunday World*. It was the story of how a teenage girl had been pushed by her father into a marriage to an elderly farmer against her will, and had been driven to the point of a nervous breakdown. It was a story of persecution, exploitation and despair. Even though no names were mentioned, Paddy and Dan recognised themselves in the rather short article. The two men who ruled their households with such absolute power were aghast. They had never in their wildest dreams reckoned that their behaviour would come under the spotlight in a newspaper report.

Pandemonium broke out in the car. In the confined space of the small vehicle, Paddy and Dan both started throwing punches and blows at Nuala, shouting abuse at her and yelling questions at the petrified pregnant teenager. 'Who did you talk to, you bitch?' 'Why did you do this?' 'How did they get this story?' 'Did they pay you for it?' Nuala protested, truthfully, that she had nothing to do with the article but in their fury the two men refused to believe her. Josey's entreaties to leave her daughter alone were ignored.

Paddy was reading out the article in the car, and after every few words he or Dan would land a punch or a slap on the weeping teenager.

Dan fumed, 'When I get the bastard that wrote that story I will kill him. Made us look like a right pair of cunts.'

All plans for a sedate Sunday outing were abandoned, and Paddy turned the car around and drove the short distance back to Dan's house. Nuala was brought into the kitchen and was not allowed to sit down. Having left the confined space of the car, Paddy and Dan could now get to work on her properly. The wailing teenager was kicked, punched and slapped by the two big men, and thrown from one to the other. Through her tears she kept proclaiming her innocence. Nuala's weeping mother tried to intervene, screaming at the two assailants to leave her daughter alone, but she was ignored. For Nuala, it was a beating she would never forget, a beating that could have killed the baby she was carrying.

At one stage, Dan grabbed his daughter by the hair and swung her down on the floor. There was a picture of the Sacred Heart in the room, with a red lamp in front of it. He shouted at her, 'Swear in front of that picture that you didn't do it. Swear, you little bitch!' Nuala swore that she didn't. Dan's mercenary frame of mind also shone through during the interrogation. He figured that his daughter had been paid handsomely for the story, and he wanted to know where the money was. He began hitting her head off the floor and shouting at her, 'You sold that story, you fucking bitch. They fucking paid you, didn't they? You must have got money for it. How much did you get? What did you do with the fucking money, you bitch?'

Dan's double-barrelled shotgun was produced, and it was made plain to Nuala that it was fully loaded. A pen and notepaper was also brought, and the text of a letter denying the newspaper story was dictated to her. To encourage her to write the letter, the barrel of the shotgun was shoved into her mouth. The letter was then posted to the *Sunday World*. To this day, Nuala cannot remember what she was told to write in the letter. She thinks the two men began to believe her when she still protested her innocence even after being threatened with the shotgun.

I remember receiving the letter – it was written on blue, lined note-paper, in big, childlike handwriting. It carried an air of indignation, and strongly denied the report that had been published, the writer stating that she was 'very happy' in her marriage. I felt I had done my homework and got the story right. I wondered if I had come up against the old Irish tradition of the cover-up, the tradition of outright denial of unpalatable truths. I had only been in journalism a few years, but had often encountered our own homespun version of the Sicilian Mafia tradition of '*omerta*'. Some of our politicians, public servants and churchmen made secretive Mafia dons look like blabbermouths. I concluded that the letter had probably been written under duress, and wondered what appalling pressure had been brought to bear on this unfortunate girl to go back on the story she had related in the hospital. However, I never dreamt that such a terrifying physical threat had been made against Nuala to 'encourage' her to pen the note.

Some time after the letter was written, Dan and Paddy left the house together. Nuala does not know where they went. They may have gone to a pub for a stiff drink. Later on that eventful Sunday, Paddy drove Nuala back to his house and locked her into the room she originally had before being forced to sleep with him. This room had a particular significance for her – it was the room where she was first raped. Despite this, she had come to love the room, because it gave her some private personal space in a house that she saw as hostile territory. Even though Paddy had torn down her David Essex posters from the walls, she had continued putting up new ones that she got from the teenage magazines that she had on order in the local shop.

Paddy locked the door and went away with the key. If Nuala had to answer a call of nature, there was a chamber pot under the bed. But Paddy didn't realise she also had a key hidden away in the room for emergencies; she had gone through all the old keys in the house until she found the right one. Even if she got out she had nowhere to go, but it was nice to know she was not a total prisoner.

She was in agony that night from the beatings. She stayed hunched in a corner of the room, lying in a foetal position on the floor, a blanket thrown over her. She wasn't able to lie on the bed or move with the pain in her ribs. She could not sleep. She stayed awake most of the night. Any time she could, she stayed awake in that house. She always had this fear that if she fell asleep the husband would rape her or something terrible would happen. Some time early the next morning she must have dozed off. The husband came in and nudged her awake with his boot. Then he went out without a word, leaving the door open. She was conscious of the birds singing in the trees outside her window.

Paddy was deeply resentful towards his young wife for a long time after the newspaper incident. She was not let out anywhere until the marks of the beatings had disappeared. No visitors were allowed into the house either, in case they might see the state she was in. Sylvester was told by Dan and Paddy that if he opened his mouth about Nuala's injuries he was dead. Nuala never saw the two of them so bitter. When Sylvester saw her injuries he was really shaken. Nuala was never aware of Sylvester being hit, but she thought he feared he might meet the same fate.

Later, she felt glad about the story in the newspaper, glad that some revenge had been taken on her two tormentors. She would have felt even better had it been her revenge instead of somebody else's. At the time, she did not want the publicity because of the immediate consequences for her. But afterwards she was delighted. She often thought of how she might get through to the reporter who wrote the article.

She thought, 'He is after exposing this scandal and I bet he will do something for me.' But she never made contact. If she had, in fact, asked me for help, I honestly don't know what I would have done. Journalists are fine at reporting on other people's problems – sorting them out is another matter.

After the exposure in the newspaper, Nuala heard that Dan became quite blatant in his boastings in the pub about how he had got a great 'catch' for his daughter, and how he had got a big cut for himself in arranging the 'match'. She learned this from Carmel, whom she always tried to see surreptitiously on visits home to her mother. Dan didn't want her mixing with schoolgirls her own age as she was now a married woman. But Nuala usually found a way of keeping up some minimal contact with Carmel and a couple of her other friends. Carmel's information came from girls who had heard their own parents talking. Knockslattery had a crude, but very effective, bush telegraph system.

It was as if Dan was showing his defiance of the outside world, as if he was saying to society, 'Yes, I sold her. What of it?' Even in Nuala's presence, he would complain to her mother, saying, 'Why didn't you have more daughters? If I had daughters instead of them sons, I would have made a fortune. There's no bloody money in boys.'

CHAPTER ELEVEN

THE BIRTH

The struggle to bring her baby into the world was long and hard and full of agony. It was a very difficult birth and it seemed to Nuala to go on forever. Finally her son was born. It should have been a joyful event for Nuala but it wasn't. It simply acted as a reminder to her that she had been raped. A smiling nun came bustling up to her with the baby peeping out from a fuzzy pink blanket and said, 'Do you want to see your son? All the roaring you did for this little child!'

Nuala shouted and screamed at the nun, 'Take it away. Get it away from me now. I don't care what you do with it. Just take it away.'

The smile froze on the nun's face. She was aghast. 'May God forgive you,' the sister murmured as she hurried away with the infant. For Nuala, the very thought of the baby at that moment just made her stomach turn.

Just a few hours before she went into labour, Nuala had taken a glorious revenge on her husband. Because it was a private hospital, she was able to have little luxuries like yoghurt, which she enjoyed. She asked the nurse to open the tops of twelve yoghurts and pour them all into a jug which she kept by her bedside. Paddy came in to visit her, and when he was within range, she let fly with the jug, drowning him and his good suit with the yoghurt. He was shocked and outraged and went as if to attack her, saying 'I'll kill ...' But he didn't finish the sentence and didn't land a blow on her either. Perhaps a respectable farmer, a 'figure of society' could not let himself down in front of nurses and medical staff. He turned on his heel and walked out. She had seldom seen him so angry – it was marvellous. It was a really sweet moment of revenge. The nurses helped to clean him up.

Her son was born that night. Paddy came in later to see her and the baby. She told him that when she threw the jug at him she had been delirious. It was a lie but he believed it. 'Thank Christ for that,' she thought. At least she would avoid a beating when she got home. Paddy thought the baby looked very dark-skinned. With his suspicious mind, he wondered if she had been with a black man. She chuckles now at the thought. 'There wasn't a black man within a hundred miles of where we lived. If I had seen a black person in the parish at that time I would have got a fright. I did not see a black person until I went to England.'

She felt that she just could not summon up interest in the baby, or feel any love for it. The nun told her she was going through post-natal depression and that she would get over it. Nuala was in the hospital ten days and during that time she did not want to see or go near her child. The babies in those days were kept in a nursery, and the other mothers would go down regularly to see their babies. They thought it very strange that she did not go to see her son. Nuala felt she just could not do it. When it came to going home, her parents and the husband came in to collect her and her son. The baby was handed to Nuala by the staff and she passed it to her mother, saying, 'You can have it. I don't want it.' Then she walked off.

Nuala's mother came and stayed with her for a while in Paddy's house while Nuala tried to come to terms with looking after a baby that she never wanted to bring into this world. She went back to stay in her own room in the house. Her mother had gone with Paddy to buy all the requisites for the baby, including the cot and the pram. No expense was spared. But still she felt that Paddy was not excited over his son, not interested in him. He never played with the baby, or talked to it, or even held it. To him, it was just a son and that was it. Sometimes, to get at Nuala, he would say it was probably some other man's bastard.

Paddy did not attend the christening. Josey and a cousin of Nuala's stood for the baby. Dan wasn't there either – he was sick at the time. Dan was delighted to have a grandchild and he doted on the little boy, Ronan. Dan would pester his daughter saying, 'When are you going to start taking an interest in this baby?' Since neither Nuala nor her husband were showing much interest in the child, Nuala's mother increasingly took over the rearing of Ronan. After a short time in Paddy's house, the baby was moved to his grandmother's home and was to be looked after full-time by Josey. Paddy had no objections.

Meanwhile, events were moving quickly in Nuala's life. Her father was becoming increasingly physically feeble, and Nuala felt herself getting stronger as a person. She knew that he did not have long for this world and vowed that the moment he passed on and was no longer a threat to her, she was going to make a break for it. She even made it clear to her mother what she planned to do. 'When he dies, I'm gone.' She began to plan how she would make the break. She could not rely on anybody else – she had to do it all by herself. She would need money to escape abroad and make a new life, and began to suss out where Paddy kept his spare cash.

She went into training like an athlete, so as to be fully ready for that moment of freedom when she would abscond. She kept herself physically in shape, cut down on drink and cigarettes and became a fitness fanatic. Every chance she got she would go out jogging. Of course, the husband had banned her from doing this, but he would not be there all the time. She wanted to be fully prepared in mind and in body for the time that she would make a break for it. That delicious dream of escape came to dominate her thoughts more and more.

Since her mother was looking after Ronan, there would be nothing to hold her back. She began to get more rebellious towards her husband. With Dan becoming increasingly frail, she knew that he could not be called in by the husband to chastise her and to impose the strength of his personality on her. She felt that with her father moving out of the equation, she had enough self-confidence to stand up to Paddy. Besides, he did not seem interested in having sex with her in the period following the birth of her baby. She began spending more and more time with her mother in her house. Paddy tried to get back at her rebelliousness by cutting off her supply of cigarettes and pocket money, but she did not care. She also felt more and more confident that she could withstand any beatings he might administer to her. When she needed money badly she would make up to Paddy, and be nice to him, but it was just a means to an end.

Nuala's mother was distraught as Dan's health began to fail. Josey was full of anxiety as her husband made various trips to hospital. Before the ambulance men would bring him out on the stretcher, Dan would put his spare cash into his pyjamas pocket, and get Josey to sew up the pocket. His attitude was that nobody was going to take his stash. Nuala wondered if he was afraid the doctors or the nurses might swipe it. Despite all the atrocities that Dan had committed against her, Josey was terrified at the thought of losing him forever. Nuala can't explain how this persecuted woman should feel like this after the awful life he had given her. Despite all the suffering that Dan had inflicted on Josey, she wanted him to cling on to life. She would become very anxious and say, 'I will have nobody when he goes.'

At the same time, Josey's fear of what Dan could do to her physically began to evaporate. Nuala began to stay with her mother during times when Dan was ill in bed at home. As usual, Dan was very demanding. Josey would be going to sleep and he would wake her up and tell her to get up and get him something or other. Even on his sick bed he could be violent. Nuala was shocked to see him throw a lemonade bottle at Josey one evening. It missed. Still, Nuala felt that Josey was achieving a sense of peace, albeit mingled with anxiety over Dan's chances of survival.

One day Nuala was travelling by bus to visit her parents' house. The bus was crowded. Most of those on board were locals or regular passengers. She had got to know all the faces. But there was a stranger on board, a man in his late twenties, with a travelling bag. She didn't think she had seen him before. When the bus arrived in Knockslattery, Nuala got off and so did the stranger. They both walked towards Nuala's family home. When he realised they were both going in the same direction, the young man looked at her quizzically.

'You're Nuala, aren't you?' he said.

'Yes. Do I know you?'

'Don't you recognise me? I'm Malachy.'

It was her brother who had emigrated to England close on thirteen years before after standing up to Dan's bullying. Now he was back for the first time to see his sick father. He would be staying only a few days. She thought it was all very sad – all those long years in exile, the result being that even your own family don't recognise you. He had become like a stranger to his own flesh and blood. Malachy was yet another victim of her father's.

When they got a chance to talk together alone, Nuala told Malachy all about her enforced marriage. Malachy shook his head in disbelief. He said that if he had known he would have come over straight away and stopped it himself. He would have stood up to his father like he did when he was a fifteen-year-old. Nuala reasoned that there was no point now in thinking what might have been. Sometimes she was tempted to brood about that day when Dan drove up the avenue to Paddy's house for the first time. If Dan hadn't had that load of coal to sell off, or if Paddy had been away that day, all the horrible things that befell her might never have happened. Then she would tell herself that there was no point in torturing herself with speculation about the past.

She could not help dwelling on 'what might have been' again when another visitor called to her family home, to see her mother. Nuala happened to be there at the time. It was Larry. From the time he had been courting Nuala, he had developed a great rapport with Josey. He would call around every Christmas to give her a box of chocolates. And if he was passing by he would occasionally drop in to say hello.

He was glad to see Nuala and she was glad to see him. They'd always liked each other, nobody could deny that. But the conversation was formal and stilted.

'How are things, Nuala?' said Larry.

'Fine, Larry.'

'Good to see you again.'

'Good to see you too.'

'That was a lovely little country church you got married in, Nuala.'

'Oh, do you know the church?'

'Well, that's where I got married myself a few weeks ago.'

Nuala suddenly felt tired and very depressed. It was the first that she had heard about the wedding. She tried to cover over her feelings, appearing casual and unconcerned on the surface, but she was really in turmoil underneath. How she wished now that it was Larry she had married, not Paddy. How she would have loved to change places with the girl who walked down the aisle with Larry.

'Congratulations, Larry. I never heard you got married. Was it to Evelyn?'

'Yes. She's a great girl. We're very happy. We have a new house now.'

They reminisced about old times and Larry revealed how Dan had sought to be reconciled with him after the relationship with Nuala came to an abrupt end. 'Some time after you broke off with me, I met your father in a pub. He was friendly. He shook me by the hand and said, "no hard feelings".'

From time to time, Dan would get up out of his sick bed to pursue his business and make deliveries. He employed local youths on a casual basis, but if Nuala was at the house visiting her mother she would be roped in to help out with the hard physical work that he was no longer able to do. It was cheaper to use Nuala. He didn't have to pay the young lads an awful lot but Nuala got nothing at all. She didn't mind too much. It got her out of the house, gave her an excuse to stay away from Paddy's place for a while. She would fill up the truck with bags of coal or firewood, or make fencing stakes in the saw mill, or cut up a tree that Dan had bought for firewood. She would also help with deliveries, do anything he wanted. It helped to pass the time.

For some reason that she cannot quite remember, Dan went out in his car, rather than the pick-up truck, to deliver a small load of coal to a local customer, a priest. Nuala went with him to do the heavy physical work of unloading the coal. She'll always remember that day. Before they set out, she had a row with her father. He was giving out to her, accusing her of not taking enough interest in the baby. Then he slapped her. That was the thing that used to annoy her about him. He found it hard to have an argument with her without hitting her. She cried into his face, wailing, 'I don't want the baby. I can't handle him.'

They travelled in silence out to the priest's house. She was boiling inside with resentment all the way following the slap he had given her. When they got to the house she unloaded the sacks of coal. Dan helped to lift the bags too, even though it was against his doctor's orders. The only kind thing Dan said to her that day was to give her a back-handed compliment on the way she unloaded the sacks. 'If you were a man, you would be brilliant.'

On their way home, he suddenly became weak at the wheel of the car. He seemed to take a seizure – possibly lifting the sacks of coal had put too much strain on his heart. Nuala yelled at him in panic, 'Stop the car, Daddy!' He managed to bring the car to a halt, falling in on top of her in a kind of faint. He gasped, 'I'm dying, Nuala.' She had heard that before. Several times in the recent past he had whimpered that he was dying but unfortunately, from her point of view, these were false alarms. Now, with a little bit of luck, she reckoned that this might be the real McCoy.

She felt a sense of relief, mixed in with some small vestige of guilt, for wishing her father dead. She thought, 'Jesus, I will now get my freedom.' The more she looked at her father getting weak, the more she felt the weight lifting off her. She could not resist lashing into him verbally, now that his aura of macho power was fading.

'You're dying now. You will never hurt me again, you bastard. You will never do again what you used to do. You're finished.' She spat the words at him with venom, and she had the feeling that she really got to him. There was nothing he could do. Suddenly she had the power. The worm had turned. At the same time, even though she had wanted her father dead for much of her life, the idea of him dying there and then on the road really frightened her. Her emotions were in turmoil – one moment she wanted him dead, the next she was doing her best to help him.

She got out of the car, shaking with nerves. She managed to man-handle her father into the passenger seat.

'I will drive you to the doctor.'

'No,' he wheezed. 'I'm in my dirty clothes. Drive me home.'

Her father's rasping breath was faltering. She feared he was going to die in the car. Then he sat up straight again and was trying to say something. He fumbled and produced a grubby cigarette packet with the names of three racehorses scrawled on it.

'These are three good things,' he gasped. 'These three horses are going to win. Before you drive me home, get me to the bookie's.'

Nuala, who was on her knees outside the car at this stage, after pulling and pushing her father into the passenger seat, could not be-lieve what she was hearing. A truck drove up behind and the driver got out, quickly realised that Dan was seriously ill, and offered to help.

Nuala almost screamed in frustration at the trucker, 'He wants me to drive him to the fucking bookie's! He's dying and he wants to shag-gin' well gamble!'

Then Nuala, whose knees were cut from the gravel, got into the driver's seat of the car. The truck driver said he would follow along behind to make sure they got home all right.

As she took the wheel, a thought hit her like a thunder clap. This was her chance. She would drive the car at high speed, crash it, and the two of them would be history. Her misery would be at an end, and this pathetic excuse for a father would also be dead. There would be a certain poetic justice about the crash. For the car that would end both their lives was the Morris Mini, that had formed part of the price Paddy had paid for her.

She could see a Stop sign ahead. Across the junction was a stone wall. She wondered if she would be able to rev up enough speed to hit it a right clatter. Hopefully, when she rammed the car into that wall, it would be a quick death. It would not make much difference to her father, she reckoned. He didn't have long to go anyway. She looked at the wall and then looked at her father. As she revved up the engine of the Mini, she said to him, 'Do you see that wall? Well, I'm going to crash into that fucking wall and kill the two of us. We are going to die now together.' She guessed that with a small car they would have little hope in a head-on collision. Her father had been in crashes before and was fearful of them.

She sensed that this man who had terrorised his family for years was now frightened himself, and was in fear of his life. At that moment she had the power of life and death over him. The tables had at last been turned on this man who had beaten her, molested her and ultimately sold her. She felt she was giving him just a small dose of his own medicine. He reached out and put his hand on hers, as if to restrain her, or to plead with her not to kill him.

Nuala wrestled with her thoughts and with her conscience and ultimately backed away from murder. Much as she was tempted to take her father's life, she could not bring herself to go through with it. She told him it was not worth taking her own life because he was going to die anyway. She didn't give a damn about him, but in another way she felt sorry for him, and in the end she just wanted to get him home and get the doctor for him.

Nuala felt fearful as she drove along the narrow country roads, her father wheezing and gasping beside her. It was reassuring to know that the truck driver was following behind. She was frightened that her father would not survive the trip, that he would die on the way. How could she drive up to the house and tell her mother there was a corpse in the car? When she got to the cottage her mother was at the door. Josey did not notice at first that her husband was ill. She said to Nuala as she jumped out of the car, 'Your father's dinner is ready.' (In rural Ireland at this time, the midday meal was usually referred to as 'dinner' rather than lunch.)

Josey was aghast when she realised that there was something wrong with her husband as he lay slumped in the car.

'What did you do to him?' she wailed accusingly at Nuala.

'Daddy is dying, Mammy,' said Nuala.

'He is not dying,' said a furious Josey, who did not want to face up to stark, frightening reality. 'How dare you say that! How dare you!'

Nuala and the truck driver helped Dan out of the car. Dan gestured to them to put him sitting on the windowsill outside the house. He gasped, 'Get me the doctor.' Nuala hurried off to find a phone.

When she came back, she told her distraught mother that the doctor and the priest were on their way. Josey became angry and agitated again, saying to the truck driver, 'She's after phoning the priest. Sure he doesn't need the priest.' Calling in the priest to give Dan the last rites was like an admission that he was at death's door. Despite all the terrible things he had done to her, the idea that her husband might be dying frightened Josey.

The trucker said to her gently, 'Ma'am, your daughter is right to call the priest.'

By now, neighbours had come to help out, and Dan had been carried into the house and put lying on a bed. He gasped to his wife, 'It's all right, I do want the priest.'

Ironically, the priest Nuala phoned was Fr McKeague, the parish priest who had stood up to Dan and refused to marry her to Paddy. When Nuala phoned him to say her father was dying, he sounded sceptical and asked her, 'Are you really sure?' Much as he disliked Dan, he still came out to anoint him. Even though Nuala hated her father, and even though she had little time for a religion that she considered had been forced down her throat at school, she still wanted to see him get the last rites.

At this stage Dan was drifting in and out of consciousness. He didn't say anything to the priest as he was being anointed. Maybe he did not want to say anything. Fr McKeague shook hands gravely with Josey as he was leaving. Even though he was silent when the priest was there, Dan was willing to talk to the doctor when he arrived. He told the doctor that everything that he had was to be given to Josey. Dan never got his bets on, and Nuala never checked to see if his three 'good things' ever won. The doctor arranged for an ambulance to take Dan into hospital. It was the last day Dan would ever hit his daughter.

Relatives gathered around as Dan lay dying in hospital. Nuala's mother was distraught, weeping all the time. Nuala went to see her father a number of times on his deathbed. She had this burning, deepseated need to talk to him about the way he had forced her into a marriage that had had such awful consequences for her. Why had he done it? How could he, as a father, even think of trying to make a profit from selling her like a slave? She hoped that when she was alone with him she might get some answers to these fundamental questions. It would be her last chance to get an explanation.

Dan was breathing through an oxygen mask and Nuala sat beside him, leaning over towards him, looking him in the eye.

'Daddy, would you like to say something to me? Would you like to say you're sorry, Daddy?'

She pulled down the mask briefly but Dan would not open his mouth. He just kept staring at her. She put the mask back on his mouth, and a few minutes later her sister Fidelma walked in. Dan said something to her, and he also talked to one of Nuala's brothers who came in. But he would not talk to Nuala.

Later that night Nuala got a friend to drive her back to the hospital. She was the only visitor. Dan was wheezing and it was clear that the end was not far away. Nuala kept saying to him, 'Can't you say something to me? Can't you say you're sorry? Please say you're sorry, Daddy, that you did this to me. You're dying now, Daddy. Please say it and I'll forgive you.' At one stage he raised his hand and touched her weakly on the cheek. She still cannot decide if this was a last attempt to slap her across the face, or a belated gesture of affection, a request for forgiveness.

It was the last time Nuala would ever see her father alive. She was desperate for her own peace of mind to get an apology from him, but he never spoke the words she wanted to hear. If he had said he was sorry, she would have forgiven him and let it all go, and would not now be telling her story. Later that night he was to slip into a coma from which he would never emerge. Nuala was the last relative to talk to him. The accusing face of his daughter was one of the last sights he saw before dropping away into oblivion.

CHAPTER TWELVE

THE ESCAPE

There was a sense of urgency about the jangling of the telephone downstairs. The noise roused her from her slumber. Nuala was still in bed in her husband's house. She checked the time. It was 6.30am. Paddy was already up. She could hear him answering the phone. She guessed what the message was. She heard him coming up the stairs. He looked into the bedroom and said, 'Your father is dead.'

It was the best news she had heard in her life. The Angel of Death had never been so welcome. She almost felt a physical weight lifting off her soul. At long last, her persecutor was gone. She knew exactly what she was going to do – she was going to do a runner. She had been in bondage for close on two years in this house and now it was all coming to an end. She had planned in her mind what she was going to do, and now the time had come to execute that plan. There was no time to lose.

She told the husband she would get up immediately and have a bath. She jumped up out of bed, and threw on jeans and a sweater. She didn't care how she looked. She was not dressing to be admired. She just wanted to get out of there. After some time, Paddy drove off in his car – she thinks it was to make arrangements for her father's funeral. Sylvester was up in the fields. She knew that she would need a size-able amount of money to make good her escape and make a new life for herself far away. She would have to pay for travel, for food, for a roof over her head as she went to ground. She needed cash to tide her over until she found a job and became financially independent. She knew that Paddy kept a significant hoard of money in a trunk, where he also stored important documents like insurance policies. It was vital that she get her hands on that money, otherwise her entire escape plan could be scuppered.

She grabbed a crowbar and quickly set to work on the locked trunk, which was kept in a corner of Paddy's bedroom. The trunk always reminded her of a treasure chest from a pirate movie. She knew she had little time. Finally she managed to prise open the lid. Inside there was a jewellery box containing a bundle of banknotes. She grabbed the cash, riffling quickly through the notes to see how much was there. She was quite pleased to find that the total came to £1,300, a lot of money back in the 1970s. There was no time for hesitation or half measures. She took the lot. 'Thanks, Paddy.' After all she had been through, she felt morally entitled to grab the money. It was payback time.

Doing everything with a sense of urgency as if her life depended on it, she packed a change of clothes, a few other essentials and, of course, the cash, into a shoulder bag. Sylvester was still away from the house. She could not risk losing time to go looking for him to say goodbye. Since he was illiterate, there was no point in leaving a note – anyway, there would have been the danger that the husband might come home early and find it. She slipped out the front door, skipped down the fine, limestone steps, and set off gently jogging down the long avenue to the main road. As she moved along, each step bringing her closer to a new life, she sang to herself, 'I'm free, I'm free, I'm free ...' She had psyched herself up, prepared herself mentally for weeks for this moment of escape. It was fear of her father that had primarily kept her in this sad, terrifying relationship. Now that her father was gone, she could at last take action.

She ran out through the big gates at the end of the avenue for what she hoped was the last time. She waited on the road for the bus. She was terrified the husband would drive up, and kept looking over her shoulder. She can't remember how long she waited. It seemed like an eternity. On this day of all days, she prayed fervently that the bus hadn't broken down or been delayed. Finally the old green bus with its growling engine lumbered slowly into view. To her, it was such a beautiful sight. She flagged it down and with a deep sense of relief stepped on board. Charley, the regular driver, was at the wheel and he gave her a friendly greeting. He knew her well – she was the girl who had often boarded his bus with bruised face and arms. He had got talking to her one day and she told him how she had got the bruises.

She found a seat at the very back of the bus and hunched down, trying to look inconspicuous. This would be the first leg of her journey into exile. Ironically, the bus route went through her home village of Knockslattery, and she felt the tension rise as her family home came into sight. She peeped out and saw the cars of relatives and family friends parked outside her mother's house. People had gathered inside the cottage paying their respects following Dan's death. Nuala thought of her mother and of the grief she must be suffering, and felt a stab of remorse, but she just had to press on with the escape. Much as she would have liked to have consoled her mother in her bereavement, there was no way she could abandon her plans now. She just had to keep on the move. Nuala glanced quickly at the cars to see if she could spot Paddy's, but it did not seem to be there. That was a relief. Going through Knockslattery was a moment of high risk. She was afraid that the husband might be around, or that a neighbour might get on the bus and that somehow the gaff would be blown. But all went well.

She travelled to a town some miles away, where she had to wait for an hour before the bus was scheduled to resume the journey. Charley chatted to her and she decided to confide in him. She needed some-body to talk to, even if it was a virtual stranger, and she felt she could trust him.

'You won't see me again,' she said.

'Why not, Nuala?'

'I'm running away.'

'Is that a fact?'

'Do you fancy a pint?'

'Why not?'

They went into a pub, and she chose the most secluded corner where few people could see them. The homely, middle-aged woman behind the bar studied them closely as she served up a pint of Guin-ness for the uniformed bus driver and a vodka for the attractive teen-age girl. They were an unusual couple. Charley paid for the drinks. As they drank, Nuala poured her heart out to him about how she had to flee, and could not even stick around for her father's funeral. Charley had always shown sympathy for her and now he listened with aston-ishment and fascination as she told of her escape plans.

He told her, 'Nuala, you're right to make your escape. But I'm also worried about you. You're only eighteen. There's a very tough world out there.'

Despite the note of caution that he sounded, his moral support made her feel a lot more at ease. Nuala ordered another vodka, 'just to steady my nerves,' but that was all. In that pub on that supremely im-portant day in her life, she disciplined herself not to drink too much. She had this awful fear that if she got really drunk she might some-how lose control and end up back in the husband's house. There was no way she could let that happen. This was the first day of the rest of her life, and nothing must be allowed to stymie her flight to freedom.

Nuala was relatively sober when she got on the bus for the next leg of her journey. She was still nervous, as the bus had to make a return journey back through Knockslattery, past her mother's house. Maybe by now the husband would be there among the mourners at the road-side cottage. Maybe he was already out looking for her, and for his money. It was logical that one of the first locations he would check would be her mother's home. This was going to be another high-risk part of the journey. As the bus approached her mother's place, Nuala again felt the anxiety well up inside her and she hunched down even deeper in her seat in the back of the bus. Luckily, nobody flagged down the bus in the village. Charley knew the risk his teenage passenger was facing, and Nuala's heart warmed to him as he put the boot down. The bus thundered past the cottage at high speed. This time, Nuala didn't even dare to peep out the window. Never had a bus travelled through the village so fast. It was like something from a movie – as if Steve McQueen himself had taken over the wheel.

When the bus got to its destination, a big town with a train station, Charley had one last conversation with his passenger. He knew that this eighteen-year-old girl was facing a daunting journey into a new life and he was quite emotional. He hugged her and wished her every good fortune.

'God speed and look after yourself,' he said.

For Nuala, it was good to have somebody say goodbye to her at this crucial moment in her life, and to show her some warmth, as she went off into exile. Charley was the only one at the time to know of her flight. Many years later, visiting her home region, she had intended to seek out Charley and thank him for his kindness on this very tense day in her life, but found that he had died.

After waving goodbye to Charley, Nuala hurried into the railway station and got on the train for Dublin. As it pulled out, she still could not relax. She was afraid something might still go wrong. The husband had most likely returned home by now, to find her and, worse still, his money missing. Maybe he had alerted the gardaí. She kept glancing nervously around her. At the railway station in Dublin, she anxiously inquired about how she could get the next available ferry to Britain. There was a sailing the next day to Holyhead, and she vowed that she would be on that ship. She found a rather rundown guest house near the railway station and spent a restless night there.

Nuala can't remember exactly how she got to the ferry port. But she has a clear recollection of standing on the deck of the ship and watching the docks receding behind her, with the smooth outline of the Dublin Mountains providing a soft, green backdrop to the grey sprawl of the city. It was a sight that generations of emigrants before her had viewed with a mixture of emotions on the voyage to a new life. Nuala had mixed feelings too. Ireland was her homeland, but in a sense it was also the sow that ate its farrow, the land where she had been oppressed. Now she was hoping that she had at last shaken off her chains and found freedom. Nuala looked at the water swirling in the wake of the ship, and thought, 'I am as free as the waves.' It was one of the loveliest feelings she ever had. She raised her hand and waved a farewell to Ireland as the coastline dropped away from view.

For the first time after fleeing from the house, she felt free. She felt nobody could find her on the ship. She just could not be that unlucky. But even while on the high seas she kept looking over her shoulder. She went into the ship's bar and ordered a treble brandy. She looked at it for a long time, and then drank it. She savoured the mellow, contented feeling the alcohol gave her.

She felt a bit lost landing at Holyhead. A customs officer remarked that she was travelling very light. She said she was just going over for a couple of days. Soon, this girl from a quiet, remote rural Irish village where everybody knew everyone else would find herself alone among strangers in one of the biggest, most impersonal cities in the world. The coach she boarded at Holyhead finally delivered her into the bustling anonymity of Victoria coach station in London. She came out of the station and stood mesmerised on the pavement, absorbing the sights around her – the roar of the traffic, the towering office buildings, the crowds.

She checked into a guest house in Victoria. She was filled with a mixture of emotions – the joy of being free, anxiety over what lay ahead, and loneliness. She missed her mother and, strangely, she also missed her baby – she had slowly come to develop feelings for him. For the first time ever in her life she was totally on her own. During her first night in that bed-and-breakfast in Victoria, she cried all night. It can be very lonely when you know nobody in a big, strange city and do not know what you are going to face. At the same time, there was a limit to her fear. The greatest fear is the fear of death, and the bottom line was that she did not fear death. She had been close to it so many times that it just did not hold any more terrors for her. There were so many times in the past when her only fear about death was that it would not come soon enough.

After a couple of nights in the bed-and-breakfast, Nuala found a job working as a maid in a big hotel. The money was meagre but the big advantage was that accommodation came with the job. She shared a room in the staff quarters with a young black woman from an African country – Nuala can't recall which one. She was called Michelle, though that wasn't really her name – it was the Anglicised version of an African name that nobody could pronounce. Michelle was older than Nuala; she had been in Britain a few years after travelling around the world, and quickly took Nuala under her wing, teaching this raw teenager from backwoods Ireland how to survive the hazards of big-city life. They were both exiles and outsiders in an alien, potentially hostile environment. This helped to forge the bond between them.

On her first day on the job, the hotel housekeeper gave Nuala a rundown of her duties. Then Nuala set out pushing a large trolley piled with linen and toiletries to clean the rooms along a corridor that seemed to stretch on forever.

Michelle came by to advise her on how to supplement her meagre wages. 'Darling, you can make tips in this business. But you have to know how to do it. Don't be over-friendly with the guests – they don't like that. But don't be really cold either. Smile at them, be polite, even if you can't stand them. If it's a guy in the room, wiggle your bum and maybe give him a flirty look. But don't strike up a conversation – let him do that if he wants to.'

Nuala was intrigued by her new friend. Michelle was a mixture of opposites. She was gentle and kind, but could be really tough when she had to be. She was streetwise, knew how to look after herself and was careful about her personal security, but could also be wild and adventurous. She was very attractive and was aged twenty-seven, but looked a lot younger. Michelle stepped in to 'mind' Nuala when the teenager had nobody to look after her. Michelle gave her a crash course in big-city survival tactics – don't trust people; don't get so sloshed in pubs or clubs that you lose control; don't go out on the town by yourself, always take a pal.

One evening Nuala came back to their room after a trip to see the big stores on Oxford Street. She was tired – and annoyed.

'Gosh, people are fierce unfriendly in this city,' she remarked to Michelle.

'All big cities are like that, love. What's the problem?'

'I was at a bus stop today and I said to a couple of other people at the stop, "Isn't it a lovely day!" And do you know what? They just ignored me. I was really hurt. I felt like saying to them, "Am I a leper or what?"'

Michelle looked at her, wide-eyed. 'Nuala, in London, you don't talk to people at bus stops, or in the Underground, or anywhere else. It's just not done.'

'Michelle, where I come from, if you were at the bus stop and didn't talk to the other people, it would be bad manners. They would think you were stuck up or something.'

'This is not a small Irish village, darling. This is London. The English are a tight-assed bunch. They get upset if a stranger talks to them. Also, you might give them the wrong impression – they might think you're trying to come on to them or are on the game or working some con. They are going to say to themselves, "Hey, what's her game?"'

Soon, Nuala had learned to behave like a native-born Londoner, cultivating an air of reserve, never making eye contact with people in the Tube or on buses, staring deadpan straight ahead into the middle distance as if nobody else was there, and never, ever, commenting on the weather to strangers, no matter if a tornado had struck or a heatwave was wiping out hundreds. She cultivated a blank, unwelcoming face like the ones she saw on the street every day.

One evening after work, Michelle said, 'Let's let our hair down. Let's go clubbing tonight.'

They went out dressed to kill, wearing mini skirts. Michelle grinned, 'Just because we're skivvies doesn't mean we can't look like stars.'

The dark-suited, muscle-bound bouncers on the door of the West End disco looked menacing.

'Holy Mother of God,' murmured Nuala. 'These fellas look dangerous. Will they even let us in?' To be turned away would be a real blow to her pride and her morale.

'Leave it to me,' said her friend.

Michelle swaggered up to the door and nodded confidently to the bouncers, who gave them the nod to pass through.

'See?' said Michelle. 'Easy. You just have to act like you own the place.'

The dark cavernous interior, the flashing disco lights, the loud, throbbing rock music, the gyrating bodies on the crowded dance floor all represented a whole new world to Nuala. It was the kind of world she had read about in her pop-music magazines. Now she was experiencing it for the first time. She was excited and fascinated. It was a long way from the Macra young farmers' dances in her homeplace, or country singer Big Tom crooning 'Gentle Mother' into a rural ballroom microphone.

'You do take a drink, don't you, Nuala?' said Michelle, shouting to be heard above the deafening music.

'Er, yeah,' Nuala replied. She thought, 'Little does she know! Do I take a drink? Is the Pope a Catholic?'

They found a booth and sat there sedately with their glasses of white wine.

A young skinhead who was clearly under the weather came over, winked at Nuala and nodded towards the dance floor. Nuala looked at Michelle, who shook her head.

The leering young man said to Michelle, 'It's her I'm asking, not you.'

'Piss off,' said Michelle. She looked him straight in the eye and held the gaze, just to show she meant it. The guy shrugged and staggered off into the crowd.

'Wanker,' murmured Michelle, glaring after him.

Nuala came to regard Michelle as her mentor and protector. One night in their room Nuala confessed that she would love a joint. Michelle said, 'I know where to get some hash. Just leave it to me, right? I don't want you messing with dealers you don't know.'

She was back within the hour, and as they each puffed a joint, Michelle looked at Nuala and said, 'What are you running away from?'

'Beg your pardon?'

'Are you in trouble with the law or something?'

'Of course not. What makes you think that?'

'You never get letters from home. You don't send letters. Nobody ever phones you from Ireland. You never phone anybody over there. You never say anything about yourself. You're a real mystery woman, darling.'

'There's nothing really to tell.'

'So you haven't murdered somebody or robbed a bank?'

'Michelle, what do you think I am!'

'I know it's none of my business, but if you're worried about something, you can tell me. We're friends, right? I won't tell anybody else. I just want you to feel that you can confide in me. I won't squeal if you have robbed Fort Knox.'

Nuala took a long pull from the joint. She thought for a while.

'Okay,' she said. 'I'll tell you the full story.'

Michelle was wide-eyed with horror as the story of the enforced marriage unfolded. They talked until the early hours. When Nuala told of being tied down and raped by the husband, Michelle said she would have shot the head off the bastard.

'If this had happened in Africa, he would have been hung, drawn and quartered. He would have been cut up and fed to the dogs. The balls would have been fed first.'

Michelle became even more protective and motherly towards Nuala when she found out what the teenager had gone through. Nuala guessed that Michelle herself had a sad past, all the time running away from something. She saw Michelle as essentially a drifter. Michelle had boyfriends, but they never lasted long, even though she would tell them she loved them. She knew she would be moving on and leaving them. Michelle used to say to Nuala, 'I'd love an Arab. If I got married it would be to an Arab. He'd only want you for a couple of nights, and then he'd go off and get another one, and you'd be left with lots of money!' That was her fantasy.

After a time, Nuala and Michelle got a small flat together in the Bayswater area of London. Nuala quickly got used to living in a cosmopolitan, multi-racial city. It was so different from her own tiny, close-knit village where everybody was white, everyone knew each other, talked with the same rural accent, came from families that had been in the area for generations, and went to Mass on Sundays. Nuala found that there were lots of different nationalities in the building where she lived, and that she was the only white tenant. She and Michelle continued working in the hotel for a while, and then did other jobs – mostly cleaning. There was plenty of work at the time.

Michelle continued to be Nuala's 'gofer' when it came to procuring soft drugs. The problem about hash from Nuala's point of view was that if she smoked it when depressed, it would drive her down even further, to an almost suicidal level. Michelle also got 'speed' for Nuala. She took it a couple of times when she wanted to do a lot of work and stay awake.

Michelle gradually became discontented. She was restless and wanted to move on.

'Nuala,' she said. 'Let's travel. We make a good team. Life is for living. There's a whole world out there. I know my way around the Continent. I've lived in Holland and France. We could be in Paris in a few hours. Train down to Dover, over to Calais and on to Gay Paree, and Bob's your bloody uncle! We could stroll by the Seine, have coffee at pavement cafés on the Boulevard St Michel, find jobs. If we got bored, we could thumb down to the Riviera, and work down there. Think of all the places we could see – Cannes, Nice, Monte Carlo. Or we could head over to Amsterdam. Maybe meet a couple of oil sheikhs. Are you up for it?'

'Oh Michelle, it's tempting, but I don't think I can handle all that travelling, just at the moment. I can only cope with so much at a time.'

'Okay. So how about we thumb up to Manchester and work there for a while?'

Nuala ultimately decided to stay on in the flat in London. She had got used to her surroundings. She and Michelle had an emotional parting. Michelle said, 'Look after yourself, love. We'll keep in touch and we'll meet again. I'll write.'

Michelle wrote a couple of times but eventually they lost contact. Nuala didn't bother with drugs after Michelle left, although she continued to drink. In later years, this was to become a serious problem for her, although of course she did not foresee that at the time. She was often sorry afterwards that she did not go travelling with Michelle. It would have been her chance to see the world.

Shortly after she had settled into her new life in London, Nuala wrote home to her mother saying she was all right, and that there was no need to worry. She did not give her address. She did not want anybody to come looking for her, even if it was out of concern for her welfare. Above all, she did not want Paddy to know her whereabouts even though at this stage he probably didn't care whether she was alive or dead. She knew her mother would not betray her, but she did not want to run any risk of somebody inadvertently letting slip her address and the information finding its way to the husband. She just wanted to go to ground for a while in the big city. She needed to be alone, to sort out her thoughts and her life. It wasn't easy. She could not forget what had happened to her in Ireland – the memories kept coming back to her. Her resentment was like a cancer, eating away at her. It might have helped her a little if her father had talked to her on his death bed. But he had said nothing, and she was still bothered that she did not get plain answers from him.

She got a job in a supermarket. It was run by a Pakistani who fancied her. She packed shelves, and was then let work on the cash register. She only stayed a few weeks. The boss started coming onto her and she left. She found work in a factory for a couple of months, packing cosmetics. She had to be up at five o'clock in the morning, and would not finish until seven in the evening. She would be exhausted, absolutely in bits, and would just fall into bed when she came home. She did other jobs too, including working in a bed-and-breakfast for a while. She never earned much as she moved from job to job, but the cash she lifted from Paddy's jewellery box helped to make life bearable. It lasted for quite a while. She could never settle down. She was restless, always on the move from job to job.

She found herself a boyfriend, this time somebody more her own age, a chap in his twenties called Declan, who had been born in Ireland. She met him in a pub one night, and was flattered by the attention he paid to her. She did not really love him – she doubted at this stage, after what she had been through, if she could get to love any man. Declan was more a companion than anything else. He was an intelligent young man, and urged her to sort out her affairs, and not just to let everything go. He reminded her that she had a son, whose future had to be looked after. She came back to Ireland with Declan – this was just over a year after she had fled. She stayed with friends of Declan's in County Cork, and made contact with the solicitor who had handled the prenuptial agreement.

It was night-time when Nuala got off the bus in Knockslattery. The trip from Cork had been tiring. The dimly-lit main street of her home village looked deserted. Apart from a mongrel scurrying down the street, there seemed to be no sign of life. Nuala didn't let that fool her. She knew that there had to be at least one or two unseen pairs of eyes observing her arrival, perhaps from behind a lace curtain. That's all that would be required for the news of the return of the prodigal daughter to spread like a bush fire. There were never any secrets in Knockslattery. Everybody would know by morning that she was home.

It was more than a year since she had fled from the husband. Nobody knew in advance that she was coming back. She walked up the path to the door of the cottage where she had been reared, and knocked. She never did have a key to the house. The door opened. Her mother stood there, frozen, transfixed to the spot. For a moment Josey looked like she had seen a ghost. Then she dissolved into tears of joy, throwing her arms around her daughter.

'Oh thank God,' said Josey. 'Thank God and his blessed mother.'

'It's been a long time, Mammy.'

'I was worried sick.'

Nuala came into the house, leaving her bag in the hall. Josey said, 'Don't make a noise now, he's asleep.'

She gently opened the door of a bedroom and there, slumbering peacefully, was Nuala's son. Nuala looked at him for a long time, taking in every detail of his hair, his nose, his chin, the way his small hands lay on the covers.

'He has grown a lot in a year, Mammy,' she whispered. 'He looks well. You've been looking after him well.'

Over a cup of tea in the kitchen, Josey said, 'Nuala, I have a crow to pluck with you.'

'What's that, Mammy?'

'You never went to your father's funeral.'

'I had to get out, Mammy. I had no choice.'

'No matter what he did, he was still your father. You should have shown some respect.'

'What respect did he ever show me? Mammy, I always told you that when he died I was gone.'

'Could you not even have gone to the removal?'

Josey and her daughter talked into the early hours. Josey told of Paddy's fury over Nuala running away. It wasn't that he missed her – far from it. He felt that he had been humiliated in the eyes of his community. It was bad for his image. Nuala stayed with her mother for a few weeks. She used to see Carmel a lot in the evenings. Carmel brought her up to date on all the gossip, and she told Carmel about life in the big city. Carmel, who now had a job, said she was dying to go to one of those discos in the West End, and to see those famous shops in Oxford Street.

Nuala got to know her little boy, and came to enjoy being with him. She would dress him, play with him, feed him and talk to him. But he was always a living reminder of dark episodes in her past. Nuala and her mother had long talks about the boy's future. Nuala felt she could not settle down and take on the full-time rearing of her son.

Nuala told her mother, 'I just can't stay here, Mammy. I have things to do but then I'll be on my way. I will keep in touch with you and Ronan, but I just cannot live in this house. There are too many reminders here, too many memories.' It was decided that it would be best if Josey were to continue looking after Ronan. Nuala was still only a teenager. She did not have a home of her own. It wasn't an imposition on Josey – she was eager to rear the boy.

In the meantime Nuala tried to sort out her legal affairs. She felt she had never fully understood the terms of the prenuptial agreement, but during meetings with the solicitor who helped to draw it up it emerged that she would be entitled to a financial settlement in the event of the marriage breaking up, provided that she waived her rights to inheriting everything after her husband died. She had a number of meetings with the solicitor, and then she had to come face to face with her husband in the solicitor's office for the final signing of the papers.

She was tense as she walked into the solicitor's premises, but relieved also that at least one chapter in her story was coming to a close. A secretary showed her into the solicitor's office. Paddy was already there. There were no greetings between them, no small talk. He glowered at her. She could feel a wave of hatred and hostility. Nuala felt that the husband could not stand handing over the money, but the alternative would have been for her to inherit everything. He didn't want that and she didn't want it either. She wished to have nothing more to do with the house or farm. She just wanted her freedom. The papers were signed. She got her settlement, and some money was put in trust for her son, to be given to him when he was twenty-one.

As they were leaving the solicitor's office, Paddy said to her, 'I hope you're satisfied. You will never enjoy a penny of that money.'

In a way, Paddy was right. She went through the money as quickly as she could. With her developing drink problem, she squandered a lot of it on booze and expensive meals. Her attitude towards the money was, 'Get rid of it.' She didn't believe that she could ever be happy with that money – it was as if there was a curse on it. Money never meant much to Nuala. She would like to have it today but only for her children. She believes there is a lot of evil in money, and that people kill and do terrible things for it. She can never forget that she was sold for money.

Nuala had another brief encounter with her husband during a court hearing in Dublin, when custody of their son was formally handed over to Josey. Nuala was staying in Cork at the time and, in line with her policy of spending her settlement money as quickly as possible, she travelled to Dublin the most expensive way – by air. In the court, the judge upbraided her and asked what kind of a mother was she, to be giving up her child. Nuala said it was difficult to explain. Then the judge called for the husband to come forward. As this elderly man approached the bench, the judge's eyes opened wide with amazement. He made no further comments critical of Nuala.

CHAPTER THIRTEEN

THE LAST VISIT

It was the summer of 1996, close on a quarter-century since the day of her wedding. It was a bright summer's day, not unlike the day that Nuala and her father first met Paddy McGorril, the man whose memory still dominated her life. The trees and the hedgerows were in full bloom as Nuala travelled through the countryside in a taxi with her good friend Marion. Nuala became more and more tense as they got closer to their destination.

Marion sensed Nuala's discomfort. She said, 'Are you really sure you want to go through with this?'

'It's something I have to do,' Nuala said.

'Okay. You've made up your mind. So just relax. No point in being uptight.'

'The roads are a lot better than they were back in the 1970s,' observed Nuala. 'Some of them were just like boreens then. And I see plenty of good houses, new cars. There's nobody around here driving beat-up bangers like Daddy used to do.'

'Sure the changes are easy to explain. There's the Celtic Tiger economy. And there's the handouts from Brussels. Nuala, you've been away too long!'

'If my father was around now, he'd be scheming hard to rip off Brussels,' said Nuala with a wry grin.

Nuala had changed with the years. Gone was the gauche, gangly teenage tomboy whose world was torn asunder by the machinations of her father. She was now a mature, worldly-wise woman, the forty-year-old mother of a family, attired soberly in an elegant dark suit and white blouse.

'This is the place,' said the taxi driver, pulling into the car park of a big, rambling country house set in well-tended gardens.

Nuala took a deep breath. Although the day was warm, she was still shivering.

'Would you like me to go in with you, love?' asked Marion.

'No,' said Nuala. 'I have to do this by myself.' But she was glad that her friend was with her that day. Marion understood everything. Marion would always stand by her and be with her. Yet this was one visit that Nuala had to make by herself.

The nurse in the reception area of the nursing home gave Nuala a bright, friendly greeting.

'I would like to visit one of your residents,' said Nuala.

'And the name?'

'Patrick McGorril.'

'Ah yes. Paddy is just finishing his lunch. He will be in the day room shortly and I will take you to meet him there. You're a daughter, I take it?'

'No, I'm his wife.'

The nurse frowned and looked confused. 'I wonder if there is some mistake,' she said. 'Perhaps you have come to the wrong nursing home. The Mr McGorril we have here is a very old man.'

'There is no mistake. My husband is in his late eighties.'

Nuala could see the nurse was wide-eyed and wondering how this could be, but she did not feel like explaining. The nurse brought Nuala to see the room where Paddy lived. It was furnished simply but comfortably, with a bed, a wardrobe and a couple of easy chairs.

Nuala sat down with the nurse and they talked. Nuala could read the nurse's mind. The nurse was dying to say to her, 'How on earth did you come to be his wife?' But she was too polite to actually ask the question. Nuala was very curious about the husband, how he was and what he looked like. She had not seen Paddy for more than twenty years, not since those tense, bitter encounters when the legal agreements to do with their separation and the custody of their child were being sorted out. The nurse told her he was very weak, and might not have much time left. The nurse then brought her to the day room. It was a big room and there were a number of old people there. Nuala stood at the entrance. And then she saw him.

He was walking around slowly like old people do. He had his back turned to her but she picked him out straight away. The nurse began to point him out but Nuala told her she didn't have to. 'That's him there,' Nuala said. He wore a check jacket and grey pants. She looked at him for a long time and then he turned around and saw her and stared at her. He never said a word, but his eyes really locked onto the woman who was still legally his wife. Nuala could tell he knew who she was. His eyes opened wide with shock and amazement at seeing her. If he had said something she might have spoken to him, but there was only silence between them. They had never had much to say to each other when they lived together. Now they had even less. The nurse murmured to her, 'I wonder does he know you?'

Nuala assured the nurse that Paddy knew her all right. 'He's staring at me, isn't he?' They were just a few feet away from each other.

The man who liked to boast that he had bought her, who had tied her down and raped her and beaten her, now seemed so weak and helpless. When Nuala saw him looking so old and frail all thoughts of a confrontation just drained away. She knew he was not long for this world. Suddenly, she no longer wanted to confront him. She had thought she would say to him, 'Why did you do these awful things to me, you bastard?' She wanted to say so many things to him. She had it all built up inside her. But when she saw him so weak, she thought, 'Leave him to God.' Half of her hated him, and the other half pitied him.

The nurse whispered to her, 'Would you like to say something to him, Mrs McGorril?' Nuala shook her head silently. She could hardly speak with the emotion. After what seemed like an eternity, Nuala, her feelings in turmoil, turned and left the room in tears. She could not bring herself to say a word to the husband whom she had just seen after a lapse of two decades. Her silence and her emotion surprised the nurse, who clearly sensed there were difficulties and mysteries here that could only be guessed at.

The nurse, detecting Nuala's distress, said gently to her that if she liked, she could take a stroll in the gardens, and think things through. If she wanted to, she could come back and have a chat with this man, her husband, whose life was drawing to a close. Nuala knew it might be her last chance to talk to the man who had so dominated her life. There were so many explanations she would like to get from him. Why did he ruin her life? Did he realise how he had driven her to the brink of suicide and robbed her of happiness and fulfilment? Did he realise that she was still haunted by what he did to her, that she was marked mentally for life? Did he have any regrets, any remorse, now that his own life was fading away? During their time together in that big old house, they had never had a proper conversation. There were so many things she wanted to ask him. Above all, she would have liked an apology.

Nuala felt confused and agitated as she took the nurse's advice and walked in the grounds. She was crying her heart out with the memory of all that had happened. Then, instinctively, she had this strange feeling of these eyes burning into her. She looked around and it was Paddy, staring at her from the window. As she walked slowly along, Paddy kept up with her, shuffling slowly along a ground-floor corridor, peering at her through the windows that lined the passage, his eyes keeping track of her every movement. What was going on in his mind? She can't even begin to guess. It was a weird, disturbing feeling, being watched by the man who had raped her all those years ago. It was almost like being stalked, but by a sad, dying creature who could no longer pose any physical threat to her. She felt he was like a shadow over her. It was strange, but she felt sad for him, despite all that had happened.

She knew she could not go back to meet him. There was no going back of any kind. She went in and told the nurse rather abruptly that she did not want to talk to her husband, and that she had to go. She felt the nurse was eager to ask the reason why, but she did not feel like explaining to her or anybody else. 'If there's anything you need to know about him, you can ask his own relatives,' she told the nurse. Nuala left her phone number, saying, 'If anything happens, I'd like to know.' She just felt she had to get out of there as quickly as possible. She turned and hurried out of the grounds, the tears streaming from her eyes, never to return. It was the last time she would ever see her rapist.

As she got into the car, she said to her friend, through her tears, 'Marion, please, get me out of here as quickly as possible. Please, Marion, let's go now.'

She wondered if the husband was frightened when he saw her. She used to tell him when she was in the depths of her anguish that she would come back and murder him. Was he wondering if his nemesis had at last caught up with him? For weeks after the visit, Nuala had nightmares, waking up in a cold sweat. All the trauma that she had been trying to forget came back to her with a vengeance. All the worst moments of her life as a teenage bride flashed before her mind, the despair, the fear, the suicide attempts, the unwanted baby, and above all the first rape. She would wake up screaming in the middle of the night, 'No, don't do this, don't do this to me. Don't tie me up.' For several nights in a row, she had a kind of vision in which she saw the face of her husband, and she would scream, 'It's him, it's him.' Her partner became very worried and urged her to seek help. She came close to having a nervous breakdown. Somehow, even though he was close to death, Paddy still had the demonic ability to torture her.

Nuala had for many years been trying to sort herself out mentally, to come to terms with her past. She had worked hard and had made some progress but, as the episode in the nursing home emphasised to her, she was still vulnerable. Life had not been easy for her over the years. After sorting out the custody of her son Ronan in the 1970s, and after bidding farewell to Knockslattery, she had tried to get on with life as best she could, living in various locations, but she was always haunted by her past.

She lived with her boyfriend Declan for a time and had children by him, but she had difficulty forming a lasting relationship. When they broke up, she met another man and went to live with him, and had children with him. She is still living with this partner and is rearing children by both relationships. They live modestly in a suburban house, in a location that she does not want to disclose. They are not well-off but they manage to get by. Her children are doing well at school, and she is proud of them.

She has kept in touch with Ronan, who lives in England. He moved there in the 1980s with his grandmother when, as a widow, she decided to go and live in London, where most of her children reside. Nuala and Ronan talk by phone from time to time. Nuala also kept in touch down through the years with her old pal Carmel. They would phone each other occasionally and talk about old times. Carmel stayed on in school until the Leaving Cert and made a career for herself, as well as marrying and raising a family. Nuala was deeply upset when Carmel died at a tragically early age in the summer of 1998. Carmel had hoped to survive long enough to see the publication of this book, but it was not to be. Former boyfriend Larry inherited a big farm and is very well-off today. He is still living happily with his wife Evelyn and they have a large family.

Nuala has been fighting the drink problem that began when she was a young bride, and has joined Alcoholics Anonymous. At the time of writing she is on the dry, and is working at coping with her alcohol dependency a day at a time. She still feels haunted by the harrowing events of her youth. She admits that there have been suicide attempts. At one stage, because of what she had been through, she was asked by the Samaritans to become one of their counsellors. She took on the voluntary, unpaid work, but just could not hack it after one of the individuals she had been dealing with committed suicide.

But life has not all been bleak. She has children on whom she dotes, and they are devoted to her. Running a busy household helps her, at least some of the time, to keep her mind from dwelling too much on the past. By organising her time well, she has been able to take part-time work outside the home. She has some close friends in whom she can confide and who have been a great help to her. Her lively sense of humour, her ability to laugh at life, has greatly helped her to survive.

The nurse was right about Paddy. He did not have long to live, only a few months. Coming up to Christmas, Nuala was in her own home helping her children open their piggy banks when the phone rang. A relative, a man of few words, gave her the news in one laconic sentence: 'You're single again.' The news of Paddy's death was the Christmas present to end all Christmas presents. She whooped with joy and piggy banks, coins, the lot, went up in the air in one spontaneous outpouring of ecstasy and delight. It was as if a huge weight had been lifted from her shoulders. She ran around the house, singing out, 'I'm free, I'm free, I'm free' – the same words she had sung when she ran out of Paddy's house all those years before. The children were mesmerised and were saying, 'Mammy, Mammy, what's wrong with you?'

Ronan, now a tall, handsome twenty-one-year-old, phoned her and he was very upset. He had travelled to Ireland from his home in England with the idea of meeting his father one last time. He had only met Paddy once before, at age eleven, when he was making his Confirmation. He had gone to see his father that day in a pub and they talked for a few minutes. The father gave him some money. Nuala felt there was no real relationship between them. Ronan had been back to Ireland on visits in recent years and had never made contact with his father – nor had his father ever tried to make contact with him. Now that Paddy was dying, Ronan deeply wanted to see him and talk to him before he passed on. But he had left it too late. If he had arrived just a day earlier, he might have talked to his father on his death bed. Who knows what he might have learned from Paddy about the events that led to his birth, and the turbulent relationship with Nuala? When he contacted the nursing home about visiting his father, the person on the other end of the line expressed sympathy, broke the news that

Paddy had just died and explained that the remains could be viewed at a nearby funeral home.

Ronan was shocked by what he saw at the undertaker's chapel, and was crying on the phone. He was very upset. He said that when he viewed his father's body it was a terrible sight. He said his father had this big gash right down his forehead as if he had fallen and injured himself. He said to Nuala, 'Oh it was terrible.' This deep wound frightened him. He said that his father did not look at peace. There was a look of shock on his face. There was also fear there. It was like somebody who had been murdered, something from a horror film. One of Nuala's brothers went to see the body and he told her the same. Even though the husband died in his bed and had received the best of nursing care, the body looked like that of somebody who had had an awful death. It was a face of horror that her brother saw, not the face of somebody at peace.

Nuala said to her partner, 'I am going to view the body,' but he warned her, 'Don't, Nuala.' He reminded her that after she had gone to see him as a living person, she almost had a breakdown and was very bad with her nerves for weeks. He said that if she were to see him as a corpse, she would just crack up again.

Ronan came to Nuala's home after the death of his father. He was anxious to talk to her on her own. Down through the years she had told him a certain amount about her relationship with his father. He knew that she had been forced into marriage. Now she told him the rest of the story, especially about the rapes. She was not sure what he knew about this – he may have learned some details from a member of her family. Anyway, he was now hearing, for the first time, a first-hand account of the rape ordeal from his own mother, and how he had been conceived through rape. Nuala describes her son as the silent type, who shows his anger through silence. Ronan said little as she related her story, but she could detect the anger building up inside him towards Paddy and Dan for what they had done to her. When she finished her story, he was silent for a time. He was clearly very moved, and trying to keep his emotions in check. Then he said, if only he had known the full truth while his father was still alive! He would have loved to have confronted both Paddy and Dan in their lifetimes. He would have liked to have got some explanations. He would have liked to have done something.

Nuala tried to explain to Ronan the reason she gave him up as a baby. She told him, 'I didn't do it because I didn't love you. I did it because I did not understand how to cope and because I was raped.' The rape was a big part of it, she told him. She explained to Ronan that it was never a question of hating him, and that she never hated him, despite things she might have blurted out as an anguished teenager. She felt at the time that she had to escape the situation she was in or she would die. And she felt that with a baby she would never be free. She had no way of getting out with a baby. Where would she go? He would have been an obstacle on the way, and she just could not have faced that obstacle. If she had kept him she would have developed a bond with him like the rest of her children, and she would not have been able to break that bond. She had had to avoid all that while she had the chance. She tried to explain all this to Ronan, as they sat together, just the two of them, in the sitting room. She saw him as having a loving personality, not aggressive, but very deep. He said very little. She thought he understood. And then he left.

Nuala had this fantasy of turning up at Paddy's funeral in a white dress and flinging a black rose, if she could find one, down on the coffin in one last gesture of contempt. Ultimately she decided it would be best to stay away from the funeral, but later she travelled to see Paddy's last resting place, in the small graveyard attached to the little country church on the main street of Dunkellin, where he had first shown her off at Sunday Mass as a young, reluctant bride. She knew it was crazy but she wept as she knelt on the grass by the grave and tried to ask him all the questions that she had wanted to put to him when he was alive. Why had he ruined her life? Why had he done these terrible things to her? Did he feel remorse?

EPILOGUE

Paddy's death did not make it easier for Nuala to forgive. On the day that she heard he had passed on, she prayed that he would go to hell. And when Ronan phoned her and was crying, she said, 'Don't cry for him. He is in hell. He is with my father in hell.' She says, 'They say that few people ever see the face of God. The husband definitely won't, nor will my father. They deserve to be in hell together. I don't go to church, but I do believe in an afterlife. I pray to God in my own way and talk to him. One of my brothers is a born-again Christian and he would phone me up in the early hours of the morning to tell me about these awful nightmares that he was having, that my father is in hell and that I am the only one stopping him getting out. I would say to him, "Well, if I am keeping him in hell, he can bloody well stay there!" My brother would be shocked and would call me the devil's worshipper.

'When the husband died, my main feeling was that I hoped he was paying for his sins. I will always hate him. I will take it to the grave with me. I have tried to forgive. I have tried to understand. I have tried to remind myself that the husband was savagely beaten himself as a boy by his own father and that this may have had a lasting effect on him. I have gone on retreat in a monastery and met the monks there to try to get the hatred out of my system. I was told that the monks will talk to you and pray over you and that you will come away feeling a sense of forgiveness towards those who have hurt you. It did not work for me. I came away still feeling hatred. One of the monks said I will take these feelings with me to the grave. I have gone to prayer meetings in the area where I live and the priests have said to me, "If you can't forgive, you can't forgive. It's no sin on your soul. Maybe when you are old, maybe then you will be able to forgive." It's more than twenty years, and I still hate him as much as I did then. They say you can forgive everything but I just don't know. I would find it easier to forgive murder. I feel I have been marked for life by what I have gone through. I live from day to day. There are times, certain dates, certain parts of the year, when it all comes back to me. I get flashbacks. The rapes will live in my memory for the rest of my days.

'I went through a slow, lingering living death with him. They would have been better off to take me out and shoot me. I used to pray that I would die. Every night I fell asleep I prayed that I would never wake up, and every chance I got I tried to kill myself. So I will never forgive him, never. If I thought for one minute that there was anybody out there going through this today, I would nearly blast the man responsible into eternity myself, because no woman should go through that, in any part of Ireland, in any part of the world. Women and men living in the wilds don't behave like that. Women in Ireland were always told they married for better or for worse. I saw my mother being badly beaten, and she just put up with it. I was told to put up with it. There is no respect in my heart for any of this nonsense. None. I have no love for the husband and none for my father. My partner goes into a church from time to time to light a candle for his dead relations and says to me, "Would you not light one too?" I always say, "No, I don't want to be a hypocrite."'

Maybe the fact that Nuala tried to find a way of forgiving is, in itself, a form of forgiveness. Maybe, in time, when she is old, some of the hatred and resentment will dissolve. As a way of trying to come to terms with her past, Nuala has been receiving counselling, and a therapist advised her to publish her story in some form, as a way of relieving the pain. As a result, in June 1997, she decided to phone the newspaper that first told of her plight more than twenty-two years earlier. Her call was put through to the desk of one of my colleagues. There was nobody at the desk, and I happened to pick up the call, and, as already outlined, Nuala found herself speaking to the author of the original article in the 1970s. She told me that the original story had only touched on the surface of the drama, and that there was much more to it.

Down through the years, ever since writing that first story, all kinds of things would remind me of Nuala's plight. If I heard of the area where she came from, or if I heard a reference to arranged marriages, or if I heard a mention of the powerful 1950s play *Sive*, by the great Kerry dramatist John B. Keane, my mind would go back to her. I remember talking to John B. when I was researching the story back in the mid-1970s. He told me that the real-life story of Nuala was eerily similar to the plot of *Sive*, which tells of the attempt by a scheming matchmaker to sell an innocent young girl in marriage to a lecherous old man. 'This poor girl's story is straight out of *Sive*,' John B. told me. The difference is that in the real-life case of Nuala, the matchmaker happened to be her own father. It was truly a case of fact being stranger than fiction.

When I received Nuala's phone call on a summery Friday afternoon, I arranged to meet her some days later. I travelled quite a long distance to a hotel where the rendezvous was to take place. After about forty minutes, there was still no sign of Nuala. I began to get worried. Had she got cold feet? Had the dark Irish code of '*omerta*', of saying nothing, cast too powerful a spell after all? I was almost on the point of leaving when a woman in her forties walked slowly and rather hesitantly into the hotel lounge. Her mood seemed calm but sombre. Our eyes met and we nodded to each other. We knew instinctively that we were the people who were supposed to meet.

She was attractive, reminding me of the actress Jessica Lange. However, I thought her features showed the ravages of a life filled with horrors that most of us can only imagine. I guessed that as a teenager she must have been stunningly beautiful. She sat down and I ordered a drink for her. Her formal education had been cut short by being sold into marriage, but as we talked it quickly became clear that she was intelligent and articulate. She had worked at educating herself. She said she still was not sure if she wanted her story published. It was a big step for her to take, even if her identity were to be protected. Even talking to me off the record, here in this hotel, was a big step! She asked that I agree to a set of ground rules before telling me her story. I would have to hold off until she was ready to have the story published. She needed time to think. Also, if the story were to be published, she did not want real names used, to protect her children.

Ultimately she agreed to assist with a two-part series that was published in the *Sunday World* in August 1997, and she also agreed to collaborate in the writing of this book. Nuala received death threats from a mystery telephone caller after her story appeared in the newspaper. The two 'villains' of the story, her father and her husband, are both dead, and she is mystified as to who would want to silence her. Despite the threats, she is glad to have gone public with her story. I was delighted when she told me that the move had given her great courage, and had boosted her self-confidence. Maybe the therapist who told her to tell her story was right after all. Maybe by talking out she had finally managed to lay to rest a few of those evil spirits from her past.

I like to think that a good mutual trust developed between Nuala and myself during our meetings and many phone calls, and that we became friends. I gradually came to know her better as a person, and while she certainly does not pretend to be a saint, I came to appreciate and enjoy her marvellous qualities – her wicked sense of humour, her kindly, outgoing nature, her feistiness, her sensitivity, her compassion and, above all, her indomitable spirit. Even though she was telling me about horrific events that drove her to the brink of suicide, and even though there were moments when she became visibly upset over certain awful memories, we were still able to have great laughs at some of the lighter moments. It was almost as if somebody who had escaped the Nazi death camps was telling of the funny side of Auschwitz or Dachau. Maybe that gallows humour, that ability to laugh even in the face of anguish and affliction, was one of the qualities that helped her to pull through. She told me once what an old neighbour had said to her, and I know exactly what he meant: 'Nuala, you never lost your sense of humour. You will always have that. They might break your heart but they will never break your spirit.'

During the research for this book, I was intrigued to visit the locations that figured in Nuala's story. I saw the site of the cottage where she grew up, the little rural church where she was married, and the isolated country house where she lived as a reluctant bride. Perhaps because I knew of the sinister events that occurred there, the house seemed to me to have a ghostly, haunted air about it. I could well imagine how a sixteen-year-old girl would have found it spooky. In another location I met Sylvester, who is alive and well, and who inquired eagerly after Nuala when I called to see him. I also talked by phone to one of Paddy's sons, and am grateful to him for his courtesy.

It may be too simplistic to brand Nuala's tormentors, her father and her husband, as monsters. They were men of their era who were not totally devoid of attractive human qualities, and who were popular in their own small rural communities. Perhaps the problem was that they went to extremes with certain traditional values and ideas. These men grew up at a time in Ireland when in some families children were virtually regarded as the possessions of their parents, when young people were expected to honour and obey their father and mother, or suffer physical violence if they didn't. In many families as well as in schools, including those run by religious orders, corporal punishment was commonplace. This was a strongly authoritarian, pre-feminist age. Many husbands expected their wives to be submissive towards them, and to provide sexual services whenever called upon to do so, without complaint. It is but a short step from some of those traditional values to the point where a man decides, in the 'daddy knows best' tradition, to select a husband for his daughter and order her to marry this man under threat of violence. It is also but a short step to the point where a husband regards his wife as a chattel to be owned and raped at will. The bad seeds of the Nuala scandal are to be found in the dark recesses of Irish society itself.

Some years ago, a very close woman friend, who was dying of cancer, said to Nuala on her death bed, 'Tell your story, Nuala. Tell the whole world what they did to you.' Close on a quarter-century after these terrible events, and after a lot of thought and much soul-searching, Nuala has at last told her story.

More True Crime from  O'BRIEN

THE GENERAL, Godfather of Crime
Paul Williams

In a twenty-year career marked by obsessive secrecy, brutality and meticulous planning, Martin Cahill netted over £40 million. He was untouchable – until a bullet from an IRA hitman ended it all.
The General tells the inside story of Ireland's most dangerous crime organisation. It reveals Cahill's bizarre personality and the activities of the Tango Squad, the special police unit that tracked him continuously.

Paperback €9.95/STG£7.99/$11.95

GANGLAND
Paul Williams

Gangland investigates who is pulling the strings behind the scenes in Irish crime. It exposes the families that form the 'Irish mafia' and examines the way in which their net has spread across the country and beyond. Compelling, chilling and unput-downable, *Gangland* gives the inside story on a dark and sinister world.

Paperback €10.15/STG£7.99/$11.95

THE JOY
Mountjoy Jail – the shocking true story of life inside
Paul Howard

A no-holds-barred account of a criminal's time in the notorious Dublin prison, as revealed to journalist Paul Howard. This extraordinary life story tells it all, revealing the disturbing reality of living behind bars: frank, shocking and brutal.

Paperback €9.95/STG£6.99/$12.95

THE BLACK WIDOW,
The Catherine Nevin Story

Niamh O'Connor

Catherine Nevin achieved instant notoriety when
she was convicted of her husband's murder in 1999.
This is the incredible story of Catherine, her friends
in high places, her desire for power and her cold-
blooded plans to have her husband killed.

Paperback €9.95/STG£6.99/$12.95

CRACKING CRIME
Jim Donovan – Forensic Detective

Niamh O'Connor

The story of the fascinating and ground-breaking
work of Dr Jim Donovan and his forensics team. As
well as outlining the history of the development of
various aspects of forensics, Irish case histories
illustrate the essential role of forensic science in
convicting serious criminals.

Paperback €11.00/STG£7.99/$9.95

Send for our full-colour catalogue